HO

MW01595695

REAv rtUrLt

Reading Human Body Language To
Understand Psychology And Dark Side Of The
Persons - How To Analyze Behavioral
Emotional Intelligence For The Mind Control

WRITTEN BY **LIAM ROBINSON**

Congratulations on downloading this ebook and thank You for doing so.

Please enjoy!

DISCLAIMER

PRINTED IN USA

MIND MASTERY SERIES

If you have come to this Book without having read the previous parts, I suggest you do so in order to have an overall reading. Below is the correct titles, if you would like to search for them on Amazon and/or Audible:

DARK PSYCHOLOGY

HOW TO MANAGE YOUR EMOTIONS AND INFLUENCE PEOPLE WITH PERSUASION. PENETRATES THE SUBCONSCIOUS MIND OF ANYONE THROUGH SECRET MANIPULATION TECHNIQUES

SECRET MANIPULATION TECHNIQUES

HOW SUBLIMINAL PSYCHOLOGY CAN PERSUADE ANYONE BY APPLYING DARK PNL IN REAL-LIFE. UNDERSTANDING TACTICS & SCHEMES TO INFLUENCE PEOPLE AND CONTROL THEIR EMOTIONS

HOW TO ANALYZE PEOPLE WITH DARK PSYCHOLOGY

A SPEED GUIDE TO READING HUMAN PERSONALITY TYPES BY ANALYZING BODY LANGUAGE. HOW DIFFERENT BEHAVIORS ARE MANIPULATED BY MIND CONTROL

TABLE OF CONTENTS

INTRODUCTION

Only a few people have the idea of how to read the minds of people in this age of technology. We are so dependent on electronic gadgets and phones that the bulk of our natural communication skills have been lost in touch. With the tremendous advancement in technology, there has been an undeniable decline in this crucial aspect of life.

Going straight into the implications and ethical issues of reading other people's minds can be easily overlooked on the brief ground that it is not a progressive idea. This is also true in a way due to the highly competitive and ruthless situation that prevails in all fields. In reality, reading the minds of people gives a lot of benefits. But the methods must be regularly learned so that the results are near-perfect. Reading minds is no easy feat as you will soon learn. The human mind is very complex and many times, even the owners of the said minds have trouble understanding themselves.

One of humanity's greatest mysteries is to uncover the truth of how to read the minds of people. If you could read the thoughts of people, you could know exactly what someone else is talking about. The strength of mind-reading tricks and strategies is really in your ability to read the actions and signs you are being sent by the other person. Here are the hidden ways of interpreting the thoughts of people through the language of the body. You have powerful intelligence if you know what a person is thinking, which can help you lead communication in your favor. If you can determine what they are thinking, you can determine what they have thought in the past, and very probably, what they will think in the future. A super power at its best.

CHAPTER ONE

HOW TO READ PEOPLE

Going straight into the implications and ethical issues of reading other people's minds can be easily overlooked on the brief ground that it is not a progressive idea. This is also true in a way due to the highly competitive and ruthless situation that prevails in all fields. In reality, reading the minds of people gives a lot of benefits. But the methods must be regularly learned so that the results are near-perfect. Here are some of the methods being explored.

It is an accepted fact that you can figure out what the person is thinking by watching a person's body language and eye movements. In reality, reading the signs of body language and eye movements is a great skill and you can do a lot of things if you take time to watch, learn, and master. Of course, many people seem to have this ability, but many of us are not paying attention to the messages that emanate through these things from other people. You certainly must start paying more attention to these things if you want to learn this ability.

Observing a person's eye movements is a good way to read their mind and very clearly determine what they are thinking at that moment. Experts have discovered that if a person looks upwards and to the left, that instantly tells you that they are attempting to create an image in their mind.

Subsequently, If a person looks up and right, you can see that he or she is trying to remember a specific image.

Another point to note is that nervous people seldom make the face a point of focus. This simply means that You cannot expect a person to look straight at you and at the face or eyes, specifically if the person is nervous or timid, even then.

Confident people, on the other hand, retain eye contact for a longer period. The same holds true for lovers.

Another avenue through which you can have a glimpse of what is happening in the minds of people is by studying facial expressions. This one might seem like a no-brainer but there are over forty-two individual muscles in the face, it is not as straightforward as you might assume.

If someone wants to get close to you, if you move closer to them, they will respond positively. they are going to stay where they are or try to get a little closer. If they Do not like the idea of you getting closer to them, they are going to retract a little or step away from the approach.

If the person agrees with you while speaking to them, their feet will be pointed at you. If you notice that their feet are turned away from you, on the contrary, you may infer that anything you say is not acceptable to them.

Similarly, people who are anxious or restless continue to shift their weight and lift their feet. When you watch a person sitting cross with his or her arms, you can quickly see that he or she is an easy-going person or in that moment, they are at ease and are not under any immediate tension.

The location of the head will also help you determine what is going through someone's mind. Tilted heads show sympathy for you. A tilted head with a smile on the face shows he or she is a friendly person or can be perceived as a flirting message. Then, when speaking, the person lowers his or her head, you can be sure he or she is trying to hide something or maybe in some cases, even tell a lie.

Many people are going to try to mimic your behavior. It means they are interested in you and they are trying to build a friendship with you. You can make any changes to your actions to test it, and if they also try to imitate these changes, you can be sure that they are very interested in you.

You should also watch the person's motion to read the mind of a man. If the individual folds their arms around their chest or crosses his or her arms, they may try to shield themselves from the effects of others. With such crossed arms, when they keep their feet wide apart, these people display their strength and establish their territory or personal space in a way. When you keep your hands on the breasts, you may say that they become impatient. We prove that they are not averse to conversations by holding their weapons behind them.

You must not be concerned with reading other people's parts. If you are too zealous, others will figure out you are trying to find out what they are talking about or trying to read them. they are going to get a little formal with you. This can ruin your friendship with individuals. Therefore, when you try to read men, you must follow a subtle approach.

How Reading People Can Help You Make More Sales

Welcome to the first chapter of' Become a Sales Guru' using NLP and hypnotic methods, here you will learn skills that will bring your sales to the next stage and boost your progress.

Consider this before we go ahead: Would you like to know why your customers make purchasing decisions? This is a very vital skill as it will help you sell to them in their own language — the best way to sell to anybody is by communicating with them in a language that only they operate with.

Want to ask some little questions that will give you the ultimate insight to please your customers best?

Want to know how exactly to make your customers feel at ease with your business and your service?

Do you want to reduce the shame of buyers?

Would you like more business to be created and more referrals?

How useful would it be to know how to use your language to prevent objections?

Would that be helpful? If yes, then please pay close attention.

First, I want to lay down some ground rules:

1. All methods will be used in an ethical manner and with dignity.
2. After reading and digesting this vital information, you are going to go and apply these skills because having all this information is useless without putting it to practice.
3. Ultimately, just have fun with it. Even if it is a win-win situation... it is just great for everyone involved

to get to understand themselves and other people better.

Agreed?

In this first installment, I would like to give you an ability that will allow you to pick up on whether or not your message gets through. This ability will allow you to become brilliant at reading people, thus anticipating objections, etc. When you find that your message is not getting through and you see that objections might be coming, you must also be able to change your tactics to still come out successful. If you can master this, then you will become a god and be respected by everyone in the sales arena.

So let's explore Sensory Acuity first of all.

What is the acuity of the senses?

The handling of sales and selling is unavoidably integral to the customer experience. The customer experience covers all that concerns your listener's interaction with you or your company or your product. While there could very easily be a ready-made one-size-fits-all blueprint for the customer experience, you would also lose a lot because the expectations of each customer for their idea of a perfect customer experience is ever-evolving. This is simply human nature.

As the expectations for customer experience change, your sales practices should too. You must actively seek out and look out for new buzzwords, new interests, new ideologies, and many other factors that will help you connect to customers better and more personally. As a seller, you must find a way to remain in the loop.

The inability to remain in the loop is one of the main reasons why many older companies fail to keep up. Many of them are unable and sometimes unwilling to keep up with the ever-evolving trends and language. Keeping up with or ahead of other retailers when it comes to customer experience and sales is necessary to stay competitive.

Okay, so when NLP first started, the founders wanted to go ahead and model the late Dr. Milton H. Erickson. Erickson was a renowned psychologist popularly recognized as the man who brought hypnosis off the stage in talent shows and parlor tricks into common medical practice.

Now, what we found about Dr. Erickson was that from moment to moment, he had an amazing ability to recognize the most subtle of changes in people. We also discovered that Erickson deeply understood that if one has enough sensory acuity, those subtle changes that have been carefully observed have meaning.

Therefore, sensory acuity involves paying attention to the person with whom you are interacting and recognizing the subtle changes that occur in their facial expressions and overall demeanor.

In learning how to do this, you will be able to know if it is time to close or if you need to create more value. You will also know if they are pleased with what you are telling them or can not wait before you quit talking to them.

Next, what you are going to look for is the following:

- **The skin color of the person:** Now when you are speaking to a customer, just go ahead and note the color shifts that happen when you are giving them details of your service or product.
- Did they have full color in their faces when you first saw them or were they more drained and pale-looking. Now as a generalization, when the face is drained of chances of color, they are not pleased with what you are saying and may feel uncomfortable or depressed. This is a quick sign that you need to change tactics and try again with another approach. Now, usually they could be possibly relaxed in your presence when their face is full of color. This is by no means a reality for everyone, but in clusters, along with everything else you find, you must take this into account and apply where useful.

- **Skin tone (the tone of the muscles under the skin)**: Go forward and note the facial muscles, they are either taut and strained or they are nice and relaxed. This can be useful to see if you feel uncomfortable or stressed by your company as the muscles of the face will react accordingly, thus creating a perfect telltale sign.

- **Breathing:** Okay so let's talk about your client's breathing. Now that is relevant because you want to know how to match a client's breathing when we talk about the study. Usually when someone is relaxed, their breathing will be on the slower side and it will seem rhythmic. On the other hand, if a person feels anxious, threatened, or cornered, then their breathing rate will become quicker to oxygenate the blood. This will in turn have the color from the face drain away as the mind will start unconsciously sending all the oxygenated blood to their legs and arms. This is an unconscious fight or flight response of the body in anticipation of battle or flight. Hence, you must be mindful of breathing and then you must follow it in sync with other signals which you will pick upon.

- **Lower lip size:** This again focuses on whether or not the person in question feels comfortable in your presence. If the lower lip is big and complete with no clear lines evident, this means that it is full of blood and they are more definitely relaxed and like what you are doing. On the other hand, if the lower lip is thin and full of lines, it might mean the opposite, so you must be very careful with your choice of words and your approach. Remember, if your customer feels comfortable and happy, they will be more likely to become repeating or returning customers as well as recommend you to other people — friends, family, co-workers etc.

- **The Eyes — Concentration and Dilation**: Last but not least, we have the eyes. Many times, people love to say that the eyes are the windows to the soul. While that might seem like a rather corny or whimsical line used to bedazzle people, it also holds a great truth that only a few are able to master and control.

- The eyes are fantastic as they are the only part of the brain we can see. As we have mentioned, the saying "the eyes are the windows to the soul" should be held dear as it can get a lot of information about what a customer is doing inside their heads. Where their eyes are going can easily tell you whether they are making images in their heads or hearing sounds, or whether they are having conflicting feelings. In no time, we are going to cover everything.

- Right now, I would like to point out concentration and dilation. If you are in a conversation with a customer and you notice they have got really large and dilated pupils, then that means they are either interested in what you are offering or they are interested in you (*wink wink*.)

- If the pupils are contracted on the other hand, it may be an indication that they are not interested in your idea or what it is you are saying to them. You must put the illumination or the position of the light source into account, of course, and this should be looked at as a group of aids working together just like everything else we've discussed, not just as one-offs. In given light conditions, a person's pupils will dilate or contract as their attitude and mood change from positive to negative and vice versa. When someone becomes excited, it is possible to have their pupils undergo dilation as high up as four times their original size.

- Now, wandering eyes might mean they are imagining what you are telling them, or it might mean you have lost their attention and you are expected to do something to get them back on track. Focused eyes may mean that they are listening attentively to you.

- Also, you must be mindful of the vocal tones and body posture of your clients.

- Is their voice strong and confident or do they sound somewhat threatened and unsure?

- Are they sitting or standing or are they free and relaxed with a closed body language?

- And how are you doing this?

Get out there and begin to notice people's shifts. Putting this into practice will help you become a great communicator because you will be able to judge whether your message gets through and when you notice it is not getting through, it allows you to change tactics and still make the sale.

More Practice, this will make you a wizard in reading people. However, it is important to put all these points in your mind as a cluster and use them all together to get the best results.

Learn How by Using Your Mind Skills

I see what you say

The idea here is that when we talk, the words we use in a conversation amount to around 40% of all the information that is transmitted and absorbed. The rest is all contact that is not verbal. We may train ourselves to perceive and document minute information from other people we communicate with. This is done by using our perception and improving our perceptual acuity skills.

We can learn how to see the facial tics, note the pauses, observe the movements of the ears, dilation of the pupils, and shifts in the color of the skin. You also get to closely observe smiles, shrugs, micro-expressions that last for tenths of a second, among many other "tells" that most people are largely unaware and that we almost never see. It seems like ESP or mind-reading is simply "reading" on the non-verbal communication of somebody. The trick is to know how these signals can be elicited and analyzed to make them relevant to us. Observing the telltale signs and interpreting them, as you will soon vibe to understand, are different parts of the puzzle.

Setting Up The Exercise

Use a standard deck of playing cards to create an exercise to enhance one's perceptual acuity. By using cards in an inventive and playful setting, we can create an impersonal context or atmosphere in which micro-expressions can be elicited, detected and used in a target card "devising."

The job of the "mind reader" —which in this case is you— is to try to find any signals that offer the card's identity when they apply to the deck's different attributes. The subject's job is not to disguise, foil or otherwise intentionally misdirect the reader's attempts to pick genuine face and body micro-expressions. They should aspire to be open and genuine. The subject aims to project a clear thought mentally, in this case, the card they have selected. There are no races or exams. It is essentially an exercise in skill-development similar to the application of scales on a piano.

Choose a ticket. No, not one!

Layer a card deck so you can not see the player head. You commence this exercise by picking a card from your subject. Make sure that everyone else gets a good look at this particular card. Next, you guide your subject to tell himself the ticket, silently. You could even encourage him to yell it to himself in silence. Inform him that the card should be pictured as vividly as possible in their mind. They can keep their eyes closed, but in the back of their mind, they can still see it. Let him extend it to a poster's length, or a museum painting, or even a billboard's size. Get him to blow the image of the card even higher. Very good. Bake the card quietly, turn it into a cheer! Have him shout it in his mind softly, and make the card's colors and details clearer, brighter. The intention here is to get that card's enhanced experience.

When they keep the card's impression, start talking about the choices you can make about the selected card's attributes. Start randomly making guesses about their card. Whether it is a red card or a black card, you must talk loudly and clearly. Be certain that when you say those distinguishing characteristics, they hear what you are saying. As you do this, search for any betraying mark, move or gesture. For example, when you say, "It might be red or maybe it is black," they might look down or their pupils might dilate when you say the card matching attribute. Or they might pause for a beat longer in their breath or eye blink rate. Continue to resist the choice's variations until you feel that you have seen an unconscious warning. Next, you ask him specifically if your choice is right when you make your choice of which color the card is. "Was that a red card?" you might say.

Then, follow with other card attributes that are combined or opposed. A face card or a numbered ticket? Odd or even, husband or wife? Whether it is black, heart or diamond, clubs and spades are green, high numbers or low numbers. Do not restrict yourself to just saying "black or white" or any such bland options.

Turn it into an expression, transform the exchange to a part of a conversation. Be sure to look out for those signs any time you mention both attributes and choose the one that seems to receive an implicit response. Declare your option and receive confirmation before progressing to the next set of choices. This helps you to understand the signs you pick up as you go, strengthening your perception and acuity in the process.

If you are uncertain which of the opposite attributes will receive a response, continue to work until you get it. It takes time and practice. For some, more of both than others but make sure that you keep at it. Keep the remaining card attributes limited until the goal card is the only remaining possibility. It is very true and natural for the signals to vary widely from person to person. However, the signals appear to be consistent once they have been identified for a given person. Do not let them know what their tell is, especially if you want to proceed with this person in this exercise. If you tell them, editing their replies, even if they do it unintentionally, will be impossible to avoid for them.

It is true that this method, as a scientific experiment, is quite flawed and almost not theoretically impossible as the essential participant —your subject — is a very unstable variable. But as an activity, it is fun to do and after you have done it, you will learn quite a couple of interesting and eye-opening things. If you are doing better than half of them right regularly, you are more effective than if by chance.

Doing more of these activities will help to increase one's perceptual acuity, not to mention one's confidence in communicating. Hypnotists, magicians, and NLP practitioners alike will build and use skills like these. Using these skills would make you look like a **reader of the mind**. This is indeed the end goal, is it not?

People-Readers Are Dealmakers

Sales consultants should reach potential customers quickly. And this means we have to be able to read people and situations well to get that first link right.

Sadly, statistics have expressly shown that 87 percent of women are able to correctly interpret body language and circumstances, and only 42% of men are able to correctly identify and discern body language.

However, if the consultant trains himself or herself to read people and adapt to what they see, the estimate may change dramatically and positively. One of the most valuable skills in sales today is the ability to read the body language of people, to know what to listen to in their voice and then to know how to respond to not just what you hear, but also what you see.

Get it right and connect with them in the appropriate way. This is a guarantee that they are going to feel relaxed conversing with you. This is one of the reasons you are leading people to want to do business with you.

As I like to name them, they all fall into one of four groups or tribes. Each tribe has a different interaction and decision-making style and different body language or hints. The ones you "press" which are close to your style and you will find them easy to sell to. The opposite will be a real challenge to market to because perhaps the exact opposite of yours is the social style and your approach to decisions. So, what is your quest for?

THE LOGIC MAN

The Logic man is the tribe of thought. This tribe wants data that they can read and think about before they make a decision. The Logic tribe is not going to make a rash decision as they prefer going away to carefully mull and think things over with as much information as possible. They are always going to have a strategy.

How do you see them?

You might feel that they are quite reserved and intense, and you might find it quite difficult to read them as they Do not show a lot of body language. This group is the hardest to "read" of the four tribes.

Possible Issues

One of the issues with dealing with the Logic Person is that they can get bogged down with specifics and procrastinate to ensure accuracy when looking for all data. We Do not like changes or surprises, so they need to be well prepared for potential problems.

Estimates from the United States claim that 60 percent of males are in the community of Logic. I Do not have any figures for other nations, sadly, but you get the idea. And this proportion can be much higher if your show is in an area with people working in the oil & gas industry.

THE ACTION MAN

This is the reverse of the theory, which is a problem for many contractors in building as they are people in action. Impatience is the secret to change. They hate info, they are fighting to fill out forms. We love challenges and are taking risks. They are determined, optimistic and decisive.

How are you finding them?

Think speed-speaking quickly, thinking fast, and moving fast. Give them some details and look at the glaze of their faces. And in making quick decisions, they are great.

Possible Problems

They may be somewhat frank or hostile as they tend to know that they are wrong. Which might mean that they are not listening well. We may also dominate somewhat.

THE FEELING INDIVIDUAL

The main concern of this tribe is how other people can affect their decision. They are also very concerned about how their own decisions will directly — and sometimes, indirectly — affect others. They are compassionate, they are typically easygoing and they are reliable as their thought process is rather easy to click into.

How are you finding them?

They will imagine how they will feel about this home for their children. We will comment on what is going to love or hate their families. As a very warm and friendly man, they can come across.

Possible Problems

They often do not want to upset people because their worries or fears may not be clear. They are not going to argue, but they may not let you know they have changed their minds. They are not assertive people, and they can be very reactive. You can be put off by the direct action or friendly consultant with a casual comment off-the-cuff.

In addition, figures from a United States-based research suggest that 65% of the female population has a preference for the Feeling tribe. Many female individuals tend to fall into this tribe.

THE FUN Man

Before they are seen, this man can often be heard. You will find enthusiastic, creative and ambitious individuals that you have not even considered. They may also have some wild ideas for decoration as well.

How do you see them?

Well, for starters, this tribe is not named fun for no reason. They are typically going to be fun, imaginative and dramatic at times. They can be very convincing and also tend to get overly excited about new ideas. These people are easy to' read' and have quite a dramatic language of the body at times. They are demanding and cheeky all at the same time.

Possible Problems

Individuals in this tribe get bored and uninterested very quickly. They are always eager to move on to new and exciting things and as such, tend to impulsively skip things they think they do not need. Some will skip through the show if they are with others and then become a distraction while the others are just trying to look around and get their bearings. They can be distracted and undisciplined easily. Not good to finish things.

Learn how to read your potential clients, determine their tribe, activate and capitalize on their strengths and weaknesses. In turn, you will make more sales, but more importantly, you will have learned how to lead the opposite tribe to want to do business with you.

CHAPTER TWO

BALANCED READING DIET

The Department of Agriculture in the United States of America has developed recommendations and models to create a balanced diet since at least 1894. The dietary experts give a convenient-to-use checklist to eat in a safe and well-balanced way with each variation of their guidelines. For other essential contributions to a healthy and successful life, this is a useful practice and one worth emulating.

Likewise, my goal is to suggest a healthy reading diet or model. Like a healthy diet that includes every day vegetables, portions of fruit, dairy, protein and grains, the reading diet will also have specific components. Instead of worrying about a daily reading schedule, as you are going to see, I encourage you to think about it every week. Nonetheless, finding time to read at least a little every day is an important component of a successful life and doing so regularly. "Regular" or as we might say, consistency is a practice shared by the top attainers in any area.

The Pieces Of A Target Reading For The Reading Diet.

These are the resources you are reading to help you achieve a life goal that is important and significant. Diet would be most successful if it is consistent and consistently concentrated for a length of time on an important topic —or set of topics. Reading intentionally towards a target will make reading more effective and will also keep you inspired.

Reading Rewarding.

Make time every day to read something that will inspire and lift your mind and attitude. This could be poetry, reading regularly or other related materials. Feeding your body with these products will lift your mind and mindset more than you probably know.

Professional Lecture.

This is the research you need to do to keep up with industry trends and knowledge for your career or profession. Most probably, these are magazines, journals, blogs and newsletters.

READING SERENDIPITOUS.

This is reading from different sources, primarily intended to give new ideas and creative thinking. This could be reading from sites that you do not normally read, following links that you receive in email, or web surfing with semi-use.

Pleasant learning.

That's all you are reading for fun! You can read much more here, of course, but do not do it at the detriment of some of the other areas above.

Seeing the beam.

This is the equivalent to our diet's snack food. This may be celebrity news, much of your consumption of social media or other light reading that does not provide much nutritional value but fills our minds (and time) and removes us from the balanced inputs our brain needs.

Some of these inputs can come from tape books, high-quality recordings, and the like, but my advice is that at least some of them are actual learning, as this phase activates our brain in very different (and helpful) ways.

Why haven't I included email here? Well, while some of the emails you read may seem to fit in the above categories, most of them are job reading and the amount we have will vary greatly depending on our jobs-and rely solely on our balanced reading diet anyway.

How to do it

Just as the balanced diet has specified portions of each of the major food groups, I recommend you have a relative plan on how much you will do each day or week of that form of reading. You will be more successful in monitoring your reading consumption by making this program. You might even consider it as calorie counting for the brain.

Here's a checklist for starting your diet. This diet is based on a weekly schedule of 10 hours of reading. Perhaps 10 hours more than you are reading now - if so, you might find yourself undernourished.

Reading 10 hours a week will make you one of the most well-read, best-informed people in your company and life in a short time. This is undeniable.

If dedicating this amount of time does not seem realistic or feasible, consider turning off the television and closing Facebook one hour a night, and most of the time will appear magically. If you are unable to meet that amount of time — or if you are reading more than this — consider the balance as a percentage rather than time elapsed.

1. Target Reading— 20 minutes / day (23 percent)
2. Inspirational Reading— 10-15 minutes / day (11-18 percent)
3. Professional Reading— 15-20 minutes / day (18-23 percent)
4. Current Reading— 10 minutes / day (11 percent)
5. Serendipitous Reading— 1 hour / week (10 percent)
6. Good Reading— 1 hour / week (10 percent)
7. Quick Reading— less than 1 hour / week* (10 percent)

Why Keep It Balanced

All of these factors make a balanced mind — and together, they provide thoughts, motivation, interactions, and imagination to help your growth creation and achievement. Just as a diet that weighs too much (or excludes a food group altogether) can cause health problems, too much of one source of learning (or the lack of others) will keep your brain from developing and working at full capacity.

PSYCHIC OBSERVATIONS- WHAT CAN YOU EXPECT FROM A PSYCHIC?

At the start of this journey for us as a "psychic" counselor, the most important concept that came into our mind was the idea that we are all here to learn something; to develop and evolve towards soul perfection. When a true psychic does their work, if you seek psychic guidance, they allow you to be aware of certain aspects of your life. The explanation of why and how psychic therapy can be so effective is that it can provide much-needed insight into your life that you would otherwise not be conscious. This lack of consciousness may be because you may be so entangled in your life's everyday activities and events that you shut down your instincts and ability to access your Higher Self. Psychics access unknown elements in nature; however, there is a secret — a decipherable code within us all that is more readily accessible to people with highly developed psychic intuition and/or with the use of other instruments of divination. Such people were either born and/or produced with a natural gift.

Once we have discovered our true path, we have decided to make it our goal to help those who seek it to discover the strength of their inner world and through spiritual practice, to Achieve Higher Consciousness. A medium (a word that does not completely describe exactly what we are doing to us) is supposed to help you understand yourself. Do not put your inner forces, experiences, or judgment in place by showing you that you can do this by yourself. A genuine intuitive psychic should be used to direct you and give you likely results based on the energy you channel while learning. You see, a prediction can change because you have the power to change it, particularly after somebody tells you they see something that is going to happen but you have the power to change it. This is especially useful if your counselor sees a potentially negative outcome in a case. This is simply an opportunity to change the possibility by modifying the situation, thoughts, behavior, reaction, or beliefs. Each conflict is just an opportunity based on your thoughts and actions to harmonize power. Not all results are automatically pre-ordered and set.

Most people need help finding their way, and when you are speaking to a professional, genuine medium, you are opening up more chances to exercise your free will to be triggered in your life as opposed to uncontrollable circumstances. Clear insights into your life can have a powerful effect on your consciousness and bring power to the very thing you want. These days, it is a much-vaunted term, but it is true. It is the quest that all souls push towards as they ride the path up to greatness (whether they know it or not).

With all that has been said, it is clear to see that what a psychic may say or see is varied. Next, you need to figure out what kind of details you are searching for. First, you should find the right medium to be able to provide this knowledge to you. Importantly, not all psychics are created equal, and this chapter assumes you have done your homework and discovered you are dealing with a knowledgeable and ethical practitioner.

Know Your Psychic

Many psychics are 100% reliable. They can tell everything, know everything, act as a psychic, a medium, an astrologer, a crystal reader, a reiki master, and so on. Many people think that psychics who pretend to be everything to everyone are most definitely neither professional nor ethical.

While that remains highly debatable, you find out precisely what's best for your psychic! Most trained psychics are going to tell you what they can and can't do. A medium may be a psychic, for example, but not all psychics are mediums. So you should search for an accredited psychic medium if you want to reach a loved one who has passed over. Each psychic is NOT a medium. Many psychics are clear-sighted (meaning clear-sighted) and have hallucinations. We have spoken to many clairvoyant psychics in our experience who can "sense" past, present or future visions. The same applies to someone who is empathetic and can "feel" the feelings of another. Most psychics can do both, but some can do very well in only one or two areas of study.

Different Methods are for Different Psychics

If the psychic is clear-sighted, empathetic, a medium, or telepathic, they will most likely make use of divination devices like Tarot, Runes, we Ching, or even numerology and astrology. The degree to which they can tell you such things will be dependent on their abilities, experience, and natural gifts. All of these factors play a role in giving you reliable psychic data during your reading, and you especially want someone who is experienced if they can support you from a higher realm based on channeling. Many psychics use devices, while some do not. It will assess their level of skill-based on how a psychic worker learned their talent and how they exercise them.

You might recall watching a somewhat popular television program where this psychic read the butts of the people (yes, their backsides). People were showing her their faces, and she was going to read them. The technique is called Rumpology and the most well known butt reader is the famous actor Sylvester Stallone's mother. Go and work it out. No one should ever judge what a person with higher consciousness is communicating with. For some, the Tarot could be butts and for others, something else. However, spiritual gifts come in all shapes and sizes not meant to be puns. We should be concerned with dominance. Psychic mastery is a skill like anything else, and anyone seeking psychic guidance would want someone to assist others with it who have mastered their ability to some degree.

Many Common Pitfalls to Look Out For

Through many years of using psychics, clairvoyants, etc., I have learned that some may be able to see certain types of things but may not be able to help you with what worries you at all. For instance, you call someone who claims to be clear-sighted and you want to know if you are going to have a reconciliation with your lover or not, and she sees you have got a new puppy and you are wearing a yellow scarf. Of course, you are instantly blown away by this seemingly useless information. Yeah, awesome. For sure, that's a gift— to be able to do that without seeing or understanding the man. So many everyday people have psychic abilities, but that does not automatically allow them to support you with a serious situation in your life that needs professional assistance or someone experienced and knowledgeable and skilled in their expertise to get you specific psychic responses channeled from Higher Consciousness.

In fact, a particular clairvoyant could see that you have a new puppy and see what is on you, but it does not mean they can see the answers you are searching for at a simpler or deeper level. Their tolerance for your issues may not suit you. We found that people who are fascinated by little stuff like that tend to believe all that a clairvoyant says when in fact their gift is a gift of actually seeing "you" and what's in your physical environment. This is an excellent ability called remote viewing, but it is, however, not a skill fit for your problem of reconciliation or goal. For certain types of readings, it is worth developing as a technique. But from that point on, the urge to "believe" everything is very high because to an inexperienced psychological advice seeker, this is amazing enough to lead you to make the mistaken assumption that this person can see "everything." And that's not consistently the case. So all this is to suggest, ask the psychic that you may call or email to spell out exactly what their expertise is, and you make the decision of whether or not this psychic is yours.

If a psychic is empathetic, they can feel the feelings/emotions of another person. If a psychic is telepathic, they can know the thoughts of another. If a psychic is clear-sighted, my dreams, they can see the past, present, and future. If a psychic is clairaudient, even sounds in their minds receive/hear information. If a psychic is clear-sensitive, it can obtain knowledge through physical sensations that are connected with you or a person you are talking about. Keep in mind that each practitioner's skill level can differ, and this is another piece of information that you would like to inquire about. How much experience are they having?

All these skills alone if untrained or at the beginning stages may not be able to assist you, but when paired with education, experience, and knowledge, you can have a unique experience with an experienced intuitive counselor that can support you in powerful ways that will assist you in your empowerment, provide informative answers to your questions and likely outcomes. Note, the findings are based on the current energy that affects you at the time of reading and that can change without a doubt. Most people have the misguided impression that there is nothing you can do to change a thing if it is meant to be. There are indeed some occurrences that happen in every life that is meant to be due to certain pre-ordained circumstances that must occur in life for the development of your soul or in many, many cases because of karmic debts and the subsequent correction of imbalances produced by the abuse of certain energies in previous lives. Then there are other life experiences where free will is at stake, and the very thing that is being checked is your own choice or action. So a psychic reading is not supposed to circumvent experience because your soul is going to endure what it needs to complete its "stopover" on this plane of existence, but a professional psychic reading will help you find what eludes you or some point you seem to overlook and help point you in the right direction. Or, your psychic may recognize a block or karmic pattern with which you have difficulty dealing. it is not just what Mom and Dad did to us as kids sometimes. Sometimes it is only motivating in and of itself to become self-conscious. Awareness of something important can have an enormous effect on a person through directed spiritual forces. It could be that very moment that turns your life into a turning point. If they can support you in this way, the real psychic spiritual counselor has done their job well. But they are not a substitute for experience, and amoral, qualified psychics would never try to make you dependent on them.

What a psychic shouldn't warn you, they should also look at what a psychic shouldn't tell you, conversely. A psychic is not supposed to tell you what choices to make. Also, exclude factors that motivate you to make your own decisions about your life from your reading. Death should never be predicted by an ethical and responsible psychic. They should not suggest making spells for you that will change the course of events or another person or influence the life of another for your benefit allegedly. Engaging in this type of activity will only give you and this medium with negative karma, and the karmic effects could be catastrophic. it is completely unethical. A psychic should never warn you that something can happen to you because it is wrong. No one else can "make" something happen to you because there are no special abilities for a spiritual agent to influence your destiny or other actions. Psychic practitioners are meant to be religious people who have chosen to support others by using spiritually formed abilities, but never choose to use those talents to raise their ego, manipulate the will of others, or emotionally rely on you. There are those forms out there. Be careful of physicians that said they are going to have to do 'energy work' on you at great cost via long meditations. This is a notorious psychological trick when telling you that you have a negative block or curse. When you meet such a medium, even if they seem to have psychic ability, do yourself a favor and instantly hang up or leave.

So, know your medium, get a clear picture of what you need to know to make the best selection. Tell the medium what they are specialized in because nobody is specializing in anything. Let them stick to what they learn or do best. Then make sure they have got training and experience. There's nothing worse than getting a psychic reading from someone who does not know what they are doing. Even if they have an undeveloped talent, that does not count for something unique. Do your homework, ask the right questions, and know a psychic practitioner's shortcomings. No one but God is true and all-knowing. Ignore anyone who makes claims of this kind. That's just for the uninformed and gullible.

Reading The woman's Unspoken Words

As we said, it is easy to talk to women as long as you are doing it right. It is clarified that 'right' means seeing yourself as worth talking to, seeing her as a potential friend to whom you are strongly attracted, and understanding what you want to get out of the first conversation. Now, it is time to look at her conversation side so you can determine if she's interested in you.

It is doubtful that a girl would come out right and say,' Oh, I fancy you! Women tend to be' mysterious' even in this age of justice. They are trying to guess you and what your play is. We are not trying to play on you some rotten trick. It is part of the ritual of courtship for people hot-wired into us. She does not deliberately try to keep you guessing. She's doing it without thought. (Well there are women's games, but I'm trying to get people to stop them. Remember: ' Games' are bad news on either side of the gender divide.)

Women, in particular, often appear to be respectful. They are being taught to be personal. That's why talking to women is pretty easy. We like speaking. If you want that to be ALL, it is a breeze.

It may be a little harder if you want a sexual relationship with her. That's why it is usually suggested that you set your target low to begin with. Speak to many attractive women without demanding more than speaking. Be their mate, the lovely guy. Yet, remember somewhere in your mind that the nice guy never becomes the lover. That's how she will always see you once you are her mate. But for training, that would be perfect.

Okay, then women's goodness and sociable. They like talking. So, how do you know if she doesn't even like you? How do you know if she is bored out of her mind before you give up and leave?

Scientists have found it hard to read the facial expressions of shy people. And the main way you can assess your reception is facial expressions. It is hypothesized that because shy people tend to avoid eye contact, they are not seeing the faces of the practice reading that the rest of us are doing. So they are missing lots of valuable information going on in any conversation.

If you want to get good with women, you will have to make good contact with your eyes. Eye contact is one of the most powerful tools to communicate with someone else. Always interact with it. The old saying' the eyes are the gateway to the soul' once again holds true.

People who are good at reading people get a glimpse from their eyes of what is happening in their minds. And people who look at your face carefully sometimes make you feel like they are looking at all of you, not just your eyes.

A woman said that she once heard one of her male students say this was what she did to his friends. "It was intense with her," he said. "It felt like she was able to see my soul!" Freaked out or not, she was fancied by that young man, and she thinks that moment of contact just fueled his attraction. Generally, it does.

This is your cue to make eye contact as much as you can as you talk to her. The more she looks at you, the more curious she is. Look at her words. Most of us have a friendly eye, a positive voice that suits all circumstances in society. Under the mask, you are searching for the gestures. Her true feelings will flash up that will cross her face so often. it is like we can't hold the mask ALL the time in place. It falls sometimes even with the best.

It takes practice to do this. Practice this with them if you have a female friend, daughter, or mother with whom you get on well. Get into the habit of looking at their faces and try to catch the momentary changes to gain insight into what they feel or think. And run it past them if you start picking up something.

'So you were irritated,' you might say. If they are willing to play this guessing game with you, they are going to tell you what they think at that moment. They may not even have known reported discomfort about their eyes. It is going to be a bit of a shock for them to say they felt it.

On the web, there are some quizzes of facial expression worth trying out. But if you are not doing well, do not be too sad. I'm pretty good at reading people, but many of their examples have been misread.

It is not an exact study, so do not expect it to be flawless. But if you can get into the ballpark somewhere and use the input process of asking to see if you are wrong, you will get better at it, and you will get better with girls as well.

It is like interpreting a mathematical equation or computer program to learn how to interpret facial expressions. You can do that. All you have to do is learn the rules.

Note, didn't say anything about what she's talking about? That's because any interaction is the least important part of it as people's words can often be misleading, altered, or even in some cases, untrue. Learn to read her face and other non-verbal clues and know whether you succeed or fall flat on your face without having to hear her say a word.

Do Associations Create Our Perceptions Of People?

Many people have heard of the saying' do not judge a book by its cover,' and yet this is what happens in particular. We see somebody wearing a certain clothing item, looking or behaving in a certain way and making a decision.

This decision is automatic and an unconscious mind result. And as a result of this cycle occurring too fast, how one comes to such a conclusion is often unclear.

What is seen, the fires of associations in the brain, and how one decides on what is seen based on those associations that are caused. Now, these comparisons are going to be valid at times and sometimes they will not be.

Conditioning

Such connections are usually the result of one's earned conditioning. And the press is one of the most powerful forces in forming people's relationships.

Family, friends, or romantic partners can also have a say in people's ego minds in the partnerships.

And then there's the world of childhood. This is another incredibly important factor in which relationships as an adult you will come to have with others.

The Ego Mind

While this section is about the interactions you can have with people, this is how the ego mind works with everything. And they do not need to be focused on what's true or functional; they can be dysfunctional and have no validity to them.

But then the ego brain, depending on whether they are practical or inspiring, does not create such connections. Because they are familiar, they are created.

This means that once something is marked as common, it is now known as what is secure. And now it is automatic instead of having to think about something and leads to less power being used.

Several years ago, when people lived in villages and were at risk of being eaten by animals: making snap judgments would not only save money, it would also save lives. And maybe this is when this ability came into being.

The Benefits

Such comparisons make life easier when it comes to reading people and making snap judgments. If there was no such potential, it would lead to all sorts of issues. Finding something that usually takes seconds from wasting minutes and even hours.

And instead of following the hints, one might even end up endangering their lives. This could be due to not being able to read the facial expression of a person or being unable to understand what might be harmful to someone carrying it.

The Halo Effect

There's something known as the halo effect. And this is where one identifies someone as having only one good characteristic as being a certain way based on them. Then this one characteristic contributes to the attribution of many other characteristics to them.

It goes on automatically and without any conscious effort needing to be made. A good example of this is when someone is found to be desirable to them. And because they are beautiful, they are typically associated as smart and even good.

How beautiful someone is has little to do with how smart or effective they are. In reality, some people who are considered to be attractive will be smart and successful, and some will not.

This also works vice versa; if someone has a characteristic that is individually or socially perceived as negative, comparisons will be made. One may see another person taking drugs and could mark them out of this one trait; to be dangerous and to have criminal tendencies.

And as the press likes to portray drug users in some way, the news will be the product of many of these interactions. Despite the reality that people from all walks of life take drugs and not everyone doing so is going to be risky or criminal.

Inaccurate Associations

Examples of incorrect comparisons are the above-mentioned. If one were to hire or date someone based on the first example or speak to or get to know someone from the second example, the assumptions could be proved to be wrong; it could lead to the creation of a new awareness.

Countries and Religions

Many relationships can be created around people from different countries or religions as a result of watching the news or reading the papers. They can also be incorrect and contribute to creating all sorts of challenges.

This can result in violence, racism, and prejudice. Here, one does not see the individual on its own, but on the connections that were established through the press. What they see are the stereotypes that are being placed onto others that the media has created in their minds.

The Younger Generation

Today's youth are often described as unruly, dangerous, and upsetting. For some of the younger people, this may be the case, but it is not an absolute truth. Nevertheless, one's mind can shape such connections by purchasing what the media says about the younger generation.

Instead, keeping an open mind and seeing every situation for what it is will be difficult. Interpretations will be made unconsciously and this will make it difficult for men and women to see otherwise.

Men And Women

A person with a muscular physique may be viewed by men and women alike as violent, tough, or unapproachable, and yet this may be far from the reality. For some, this will be valid, but it will not apply to all of them.

It can be associated with attractive women as being vain and aloof. This can be wide of the mark when in fact. This will be the case for some women, but, again, not all of them.

Absolute Meaning

The ego-mind works in absolute meaning, i.e it is either black or white. There's no middle ground with this brain, no gray area. And this means that the ego brain wants to either see these similarities or edit and refute anything that goes against them.

Another thing that can happen is that the ego brain interprets truth in a way that matches these associations. And this may include projection use. This is completely protected by Anais Nin's statement "We do not see the world as it is, we see the world as we are."

Awareness

The ego brain often perceives the present based on the past or a past combination. And that's why an understanding of how the ego mind works is critical. They do have what is known as intuition, instincts, and hunches, and this may be another way to reach conclusions and make quick decisions.

Associations promote life and save a great deal of time and resources. By being conscious of and challenging these connections, instead of being influenced through them, one will be able to have a choice.

CHAPTER THREE

EFFECTIVELY DEVELOPING PEOPLE

As a leader, one of our responsibilities is to cultivate people. Yes, I believe it is one of the cornerstones of excellent leadership. Developing people effectively accomplishes many important tasks for us and our company.

We are contributing to their importance as we grow others. They are becoming more flexible, successful and optimistic. As the knowledge base of an individual grows and their ability to assess circumstances correctly improves, their ability to solve innovative problems increases. As you as an individual help another individual to bloom and grow into their full potential, so also will they turn around and give returns that not only benefit them, but also benefit you.

When their breadth of knowledge and skills increases, so does their work's pride. And pride in work and craftsmanship leads to higher performance, greater innovation, and the ability to go the "extra mile" in pursuit of excellence. It also improves their willingness to accept further duties. You will find their development potential is growing, and their possibility of becoming a leader, as you have also worked hard to become, is getting closer to reality.

When we display an interest in other people's growth and prosperity, they become more loyal to us in turn. In general, humans tend to reciprocate acts of favours with loyalty, trust, and even the slightest sentimental connections. Being interested in other people's success allows them to take an interest in our performance in turn. As a leader, it is vital to be valued and to a large and necessary extent, respected, by our team members. This respect is nurtured by the successful creation and impartation of knowledge and value unto others.

As we help the growth of others, there are even more direct benefits for us as leaders beyond simple indirect benefits. We build the opportunity to delegate more and more as we increase the capacity of our team members. The more we can delegate, the more time and effort we can manage. Delegation results in higher productivity. Therefore, the more we can delegate our jobs, the easier it will be for us to rise above the grind of always working "in" our company and spend time "on" our business. One of the things that keep us from bringing our company or profession in new directions is not spending enough time leaving our busyness to see the bigger picture. Delegating effectively helps us to take that step away.

In addition to increasing our effectiveness and perspective, as we grow them, we also bring them closer to taking up their own leadership roles. This means that we are training someone to take over from us and our duties. This may seem like a stupid thing to do at first glance by making us somewhat replaceable or dispensable, but it helps us to "fill in" easily behind us, which in turn makes us more "promotable." If nobody else can do our job, we will not be able to move on to through and better opportunities. This is an outlook that is necessary for teamwork and individual growth.

Okay, now that we have developed the value and wisdom in making the extra effort to cultivate other people, let's talk about how to do that. How are we improving others effectively? One of the problems of successfully creating people is that design is not a science but an art. To get good at it, it takes a bit of talent and judgment. The ability to read people and understand their strengths and weaknesses requires successful growth. It needs the decision to know which areas to improve a person in, which tasks to assign to certain good candidates, and how hard it is to drive the development of someone. It takes quite a lot of effort and skill to be attentive to the actions of the other person to decide whether to ask them if they want to take on something different and simply put the new task in their lap. The entire process can be divided into which tasks to delegate and then thereafter, determining how to delegate to whom.

Let's start by discussing the tasks or duties to be delegated. They fall into two groups-those requiring no judgment (like writing a report) and those requiring judgment. Activities that do not require judgment are always successfully delegated to candidates.

Key points to be successful in delegating these tasks are:

1. Ensuring that you choose the right person
2. Ensuring that they have the right tools, drive, and knowledge
3. Communicating the timeline and level of importance. Tasks or duties that require judgment are great vehicles to build someone that goes beyond the basics of "simply getting the job done."

You should carefully select these tasks/responsibilities to:

1. Avoid damaging the self-confidence of the individual
2. Not create problems if the person being formed shows poor judgment.

Until you assign a challenging task, you will need to gauge the level of self-confidence of the individual.

How do you make sure your company is not harmed by a mistake? Two suggestions:

1. do not delegate anything too important
2. If delegating something that needs judgment, make sure that you monitor their progress periodically and always leave sufficient time for analysis and clarification before submitting the results to others. This might mean that the task or job you have handed to them requires supervision from you or another qualified individual. This means that it will not only take their time but yours as well.

It depends on the job and where a person is in their skill level, state of mind, ability to change, level of self-confidence and their self-image to decide how to delegate and to whom to delegate. Someone who lacks self-confidence or just starts on their path of development needs more support and 'hand-holding' than someone who is seasoned and has already developed a greater level of trust. Sometimes, it is necessary to ask people if they are open to learning something new or taking on more responsibility. Note, making sure they are open to development and expanding outside their current state or present comfort zone is a key to cultivating others effectively. All too often, they trust in others more than they believe in themselves, and as such, they may be driven harder and faster than they want. Although stretching people is necessary, we do not want to break them. This is part of the "culture" of creating others effectively. It is worthy to note that breaking an individual in hopes of "building" them up may do more harm than good. While it is said that pushing people to rock bottom helps them push harder to the top, there are truly better ways to improve an individual.

The amount of discretion that you expect someone to make will depend on their level of experience and track record of making good decisions and making good choices. Placing someone in a position to make choices in an area they are unfamiliar with provides an opportunity for developing, teaching and mentoring. Only make sure you use the opportunity to teach and tutor, without criticism or belittlement. Do not respond to errors or poor judgment with harshness or the aim to belittle. New and/or difficult circumstances give us great opportunities for teaching. An ideal way to teach and improve in your leadership is to follow a "coach-like" approach. Rather than asking or questioning the other person, direct and share perspectives. Be a partner or advisor, not a director or leader.

Through improving their development skills by becoming an active delegator, correctly evaluating others, and implementing a coach-like approach, you can help others evolve, add value, enhance their self-confidence, and promote your interests as well. Developing others successfully will move you to outstanding leadership.

How to Read a Person from Their Personal Hygiene

The first form of communication we send to people we meet is our presence. The person who sees you will have made some general assumptions about your character within the first five seconds or so of seeing you based on how you look. Your grooming and physical appearance naturally provides a wealth of information about who you are and what your personality could be. Hygiene will reveal the social appeal, laziness, intellect, social class, education, self-acceptance rate, culture, and organization of an individual.

You may be told by a lack of proper grooming that a person is lazy. One may assume that they do not want to make an effort to clean themselves up and look presentable to everyone else, and this, in turn, will reflect on their ability to also ably present other aspects of their lives, including their work ethics.

This could be very bad. Be vigilant with this one because there are cultures out there for which this does not apply and you will have to understand the cultural background of the individual in question. Nevertheless, children growing up in poverty are typically not taught the basics of personal hygiene from experience in an American environment.

Other times, **it could be mental illness at play**. There is a lack of proper hygiene among those who are stressed because they no longer have the energy or the desire to look presentable. Those with other persistent forms of mental illness such as depression, certain phobias, and Alzheimer's disease may also have poor hygiene, as they may not be able to understand the concept of proper hygiene.

It could be drug or alcohol misuse. People who abuse alcohol or drugs regularly will often have muddled complexions and a disheveled look. These same people are also often found suffering from depression.

It could be a medical problem. People who have suffered a traumatic injury or who have some kind of medical problem that restricts their mobility can lack proper hygiene.

They could be socially inept. Someone who has a lack of proper hygiene going around in public may have a poor level of social intelligence. They live in their world and can't have a good relationship with others or they do not know how others see them. Typically these styles are interpersonal errors.

They could also be self-centered. Someone who cares very little about the impact of their lack of hygiene on both themselves and the people around them. Neither do they care about how others consider them which goes to show that they indeed have a very stubborn, self-centered personality. They do what they want when they want, and how they want, irrespective of what others say.

HEAD-TO-BOTTOM HYGIENE EVALUATION

When assessing a person, scan them from top to bottom and pay close attention to hygiene when doing so.

Hair / Scalp.

Our hair is the primary characteristic of our body that we can alter explicitly and project our image into the world for others to see. That's why the army shaves their recruits ' heads so they lose their sense of individuality and look the same instead. Is your hair groomed? Is your skin clean or unwashed and greasy? Generally, dirty hair means the person does not shower or has not showered.

Eye. Face, eye.

For females, skin hygiene should be weighed more heavily because they place a high degree of importance on their faces. If it is a guy, how do you hold your facial hair? Make-up or no woman make-up? How clean do your teeth look? Do they have any teeth that are dirty or stained? Do they have teeth / broken teeth that are missing? Have they trimmed their eyebrows? Does it look like they wash their faces often? Are there overgrown hairs in the nose? Should they wash their eyes and nose from the junk?

Weight.

Weight tells a lot about both the person's fitness level, look-out treatment, self-esteem level, and eating habits. There are very few people out there who are eager to wake up every morning to be bulging in the stomach. The real question is why they do not do anything about it.

Wind. The wind.

Does their breath stink? This may be a symptom of not always brushing their teeth, having poor eating habits, suffering from anxiety, or having a medical condition. These conditions may include some cancers, and others such as metabolic disorders, which may cause a distinctive breath odor as a result of chemicals they produce. The medical term for bad breath is known as halitosis and truly, may occur due to varied reasons.

Clothing.

A good indicator of character is what we wear. Did their clothes look dirty or clean? Did their clothing seem to emit some offensive smells or odors? What is the state of the clothes they wear— beyond fashion trends? Many times, assessing an individual through their clothing must go beyond whether they conform to fashion trends or not. Simply wearing clean, groomed clothes indicates more than merely following trends.

Body Odor.

Did you perceive any offensive smells from their body while they were around you? If so, it may mean that they never shower and do not use deodorant. Beware of cultural differences where a strong body odor is appropriate.

Hands.

Did you notice that their hands looked dirty? If so, you might wonder why they were dirty in the first place.

Perhaps they had just been doing some research and lacked the care what time to wash their hands?

Nails of the hands.

Have their fingernails been clipped and kept? Did their fingernails appear dirty or ungroomed? Maintenance of the fingernail tells a lot about the attention to detail of the individual.

Identifying Coherence Standards Any measure of poor grooming in itself should not speak for both the person's character itself. A person you meet may have a logical reason to have dirty hands but seems clean in any other way. Maybe the individual in question works as a mechanic. You want to look for several signs of a lack of hygiene, which is called reliability when you are looking for a lack of hygiene.

Effective Reading's Strategies

Anyone needs to read regularly. It will help develop one's intelligence, skills, and behavior. It is often achieved by different groups of people for different purposes. Others learn to advance their knowledge; some do it to develop their language skills; others do it simply for the fun of it. Whatever the reason, the habit helps everybody in many ways to improve their personality. As you might know, personal intellectual development is an aspect of growth that one must never neglect.

Generally, students and scholars pay little attention to determining how poorly they are learning. In normal cases, they do not determine how well they can boost their reading speed. Reading speed could lead to improved reading performance. Learning to read well is an essential skill that should be regularly learned by every academic.

The reading habit allows everybody in many ways to build up their personality. The first thing to do is to choose the best text or content to read.

When it comes to studying for school, students in general might find that it is difficult to read for academic purposes. Students should focus on knowing the material's content in depth.

On the other hand, when reading for leisure, reading appears to be light and fun. The latter needs less focus and can be done at an average rate of 100-200 words per minute. A key element of successful reading comprehension is prior knowledge of the subject.

Many people have a tradition of learning word by word. Instead of just reading words, it is better to focus on reading phrases. Reading the content as phrases allows the mind to interpret the feedback from reading as' ideas or phrases.'

Reading methods

There are various types of reading techniques. To boost the speed, skimming, scanning, or previewing should be used as a reading technique. The approach should be chosen as the request for reading material and purpose.

Skimming

This method of reading, a person reads quickly to capture the main points. The reader reads quickly in this process to get a general idea. By reading it from first to last and word to word, the reader understands the entire text. Up to 1000 words per minute can be read by this technique. In this process, the main ideas of a text are gathered by reading first and last chapters, theme sentences, and other sections such as names, abstracts, section description, photo captions, and so on. In skimming, the practice is to decide whether to read or not, what to read carefully, and where to begin. Until you find the time to diligently read it, skimming through a text will help you better understand the content.

Scanning

When you want to find out a particular piece of information, the custom is to read through it quickly. It is a tool that anyone can use without reading the entire text to find out specific information, facts or ideas. Up to 1,500 words per minute can be read. The object of scanning a text is to determine the material's relevance. Until skimming, scanning must be completed. It will help you determine if a product is carrying the reader's information. Once an asset is scanned, further information can be skimmed.

Surface reading

Surface reading is another reading method. It is used from the text you read to seek the' data words.' Half of a material's words are words of "knowledge." We make sense of the content on their own. In it, the other words work like glue and paint. They have relations but are not essential to decide the purpose. Concentrating on words of knowledge will allow you to learn more quickly. The interpretation is also going to be better. The purpose of this style of reading is to pay more attention to what the writer is trying to say.

Extensive reading

Extensive reading is reading a longer message, often with a focus on overall meaning for pleasure. But for detailed information, intensive reading is reading a short text. The reading of phrases is another method.

Rapid Reading process

The reading process results in a sequence of eye jerks called' fixations.' The eyes take words of comprehension during fixations. In each focus, slow readers take in just one or two words. Through words by constant training in each fixation. In each fixation, you will be able to collect more words. So, without eye jerks, you have to practice reading the sentences, but with smooth eye movement from one to another. This technique can be done with conscious effort.

It is good to learn to mark important points in the text. Underlining or highlighting key words, and making margin notes, etc., can improve reading speed. Having marks in texts such as highlighting the phrases will help you improve your focus, recognise key points and make the book easier to review if you prefer.

Also having other things to consider helps learning comprehension. it is what you do in taking note of the essential points. Note-taking will help you gain a deeper understanding and analysis of the text you are reading or listening to. It can help you quickly recall what you've learned and remember. Another way to improve their overall understanding of text is to explain what the reader has experienced.

Language skills will allow you to better read. On the other hand, reading will improve the language skills. Mastering the basic 3,000 words or more, which make up about 80% of the English texts you usually use, will easily help you to read, understand and learn any content on any subject in English. Extensive learning, comprehension skills, listening fluency, and developing vocabulary are all essential components of knowledge advancement.

Good readers can become better students with clear goals for reading. I frequently determine whether their goals are met by the text and their reading practice. Until reading, better readers check the message. We get to know what the document structure is and what sections of the text are important to them. Great readers can predict what will happen. We decide carefully what to read, what to read quickly, what to read again, what not to read, and so on. Good readers read various texts differently. They assess the quality and meaning of the text and respond intelligently to the text.

Problem of Bad Reading

Several times when reading tarot cards for people on the site, we notice people complaining about "poor reading." By that, they usually mean the psychic pulled so-called "negative" cards, like the Devil, The Tower of the Ten of Swords, in answer to their question.

First of all, you need to know that an "evil" reading is not there. Generally, "evil" means the reader has pulled cards that do not agree with your idea of what should be the right answer to your question. Many of the "evil" cards are switching cards. Many people are afraid and resisting change because we all have a profound fear of the unknown.

There are a couple of cards in the Tarot that we know put the fear of God in trembling clients. These include the Tower, the Devil coin, the Swords' As, the Swords ' Ten, and the Swords ' Nine.

Of all of them, perhaps the worst, the Ten of Swords, in terms of sheer bad luck, may signify another person's brutality. Typically, the Ten of Swords shows a curious twist of fate as well as wrestling control of your life into the hands of another.

On the other hand, the Nine of Swords suggests an emotional anguish that the questioner can perpetrate. In other words, by hanging on to a disaster or an emotional drama from the past, you can do it for yourself. This card is lucky in some ways as it shows that you are holding the key to your mental prison and ultimately, you also have the power to let yourself out. It must be understood that there is still hope for the person being read to regain control over his or her life when they see the Nine of Swords in a reading. This usually indicates that someone else voluntarily gives up or gives control. This is very different from the Ten of Swords, which suggests that the questioner is more vulnerable, may suffer a real loss or may be the object of actual cruelty.

The Ace of Swords controls Saturn, the world of order and limits. While this card may be a loss, it is also a card that bodes a matter's swift and just conclusion. Together with the Ace of Swords, there is generally no great suffering although the changes it can bring can be a little shocking to the questioner's nervous system. Interestingly, the card also has an optimistic twist in the sense that it can mean you've paid your Karma Bank a huge debt. In the end, the Ace of Swords is a switch. This move is usually the right one for you, for good or worse.

It is not always the Devil card that bodes gloom and doom. It means fun and games at times. This reflects human nature's most playful component. This reflects the Deadly Sins of all Seven. If you do not like things like food, sex and materials, you might see the devil card as bad. In a reading of love, it can mean that a marriage or the start of an affair will eventually be finished. It can also be seen in a business reading as a positive coin, as it can signify a contract being signed. It can also reflect a strategic move about to be made that is, in fact, to the benefit of one. Since it is a card that reflects humanity and the victory of man over nature (often interpreted as the actions of God by many), it bodes well for imagination, innovation and ingenuity.

Even where the card is put in the set, the magnitude of its significance can be greatly affected. For example, when you ask if you should have an affair with a married man and pull the Devil card in the immediate future, that card would be good news for you. Nonetheless, if you were the wife asking, the answer would have more negative implications, "is my husband cheating on me." It can mean the failure of a situation for the better when you remove the Tower card, however constructive cards surround this. If the Tower card is in the place representing "how others see you," you may simply be a queen of drama rather than face some real trouble in your life.

Therefore, it is important not to jump conclusions or react immediately if the psychic appears to pull a card with a reputation as a' bad card.' Such cards are cloud-like. Many of them are decorated with gold.

Even, after reading it is important to remember that what you are hearing isn't actually "absolutely gospel." Tarot's main purpose is to allow you to conceptualize the situation, and even if you get "bad cards," you've got the chance to plan for these changes, or even in some cases, avoid them completely.

There's no such thing as a "poor" reading, and if you are afraid of a reading performance, there's no point in being tortured. Some people are so afraid of the so-called "evil" Tarot cards that they manifest them as the psychic may add to their hopes and fears in the series. The best thing to do is ask the question and then be ready to be responsible for your card reactions as the psychic is not ethically or morally "reliable" to experience your discomfort or annoyance.

Asking a Tarot question is the best way to get the most accurate answer without doubt, urge or anxiety attached to the matter.

Did you like this eBook, or did you find it interesting, until now?

Your support really makes a difference! I would be very grateful if you would publish an exhaustive review on **Amazon.** *All reviews are read personally, so that I can get real feedback and make this book (and the whole series) even better.*

Thanks again for your support!

CHAPTER FOUR

BODY LANGUAGE SPEAKS WITHOUT WORDS

Our non-verbal and body language is one of the most important forms of communication we use in our day-to-day experiences. It is the mode of communication that ignites the emotions and responses of our "good level." Studies have shown that having an understanding of the language of the body improves one's potential to be effective out of any given situation.

Have you ever looked at a couple sitting together and had a sense of how good or bad their relationship was in minutes? Have you ever noticed how easily without any direct interaction you were able to come to this conclusion? Whether you know it or not, we spend our days listening to the non-verbal signals of people interpreted by their body language and drawing conclusions from our assumptions about them.

The language of the body reveals the truth that we conceal from the world in the words, including how we think about ourselves, our relationships and our circumstances. The people we associate with can evaluate our motives, the nature of our relationships, how masterful we are in any given situation, our level of trust, and what our true motivations and interests are through our eye contact, movements, body position, and facial expressions.

In the emotional response it produces, the influence of body language is found. In nearly every situation, emotions influence decisions and reactions. Non-verbal signals activate emotions that define an individual's core resources such as: truthfulness, trustworthiness, honesty, level of skill, and ability to lead. The perception of these signals will decide who we are going to meet, the work we are being hired for, what level of success we eventually go on to have, and who can be elected into influential political positions.

Why aren't we spending years studying and improving successful body language skills with such an important skill? The truth is that most people underestimate the importance of body language before they try a deeper understanding of human conduct in a personal relationship or in a competitive business situation to gain an edge.

Being an expert and a master in perception, interpretation, and use of body language provides the keys for people to perceive the context behind particular movements and body movement, as well as to provide an understanding of how to effectively convey and express messages while communicating with others. As a result, there is a substantial increase in overall success of interpersonal relationships.

Understanding the basic understanding of the two core body language styles

- open presence
- closed presence

Understanding both styles is the best way to start this mastery cycle.

The closed presence

The closed presence body language style is found in individuals that fold their body around the centerline of the body, running straight from the top of the head to the feet down the middle of the body. The physical characteristics that generate this form of appearance are feet placed close to each other, arms held close to the body, hands crossed on the body and held together in front of the body, small hand movements kept close to the body, shoulders rolled back, and eyes focused below eye level.

The signals sent to the world by the body language in the form of closed presence are a lack of trust, low self-esteem, lack of capability, and lack of experience. In extreme cases, the message of wanting to be invisible can even be produced or perceived. The consequences of this type of body language on the person projecting may range from actually not receiving the best possible opportunities to a worst case scenario of harboring a self-fulfilling perception of victimization.

The accessible presence

The accessible presence, by comparison, is featured in individuals who create a sense of authority, energy, and leadership by projecting mastery of confidence, achievement, strength, and ability. The physical characteristics include open hand movements used in conversation, keeping elbows away from the body, centerline holding away from the body, straight stances, shoulders held back, and eyes focused on their listeners ' eye level. Such people are seen as beautiful, efficient, smart, attractive, and they easily seem to be accomplished and have achieved a lot. We see this type of body language as the "leaders' body language."

The aim is eye contact to enhance the language of the body and to begin projecting an open presence. One of the most important communication methods we possess is eye contact. You can change the way people see them by using direct eye contact when communicating with others. Once people start speaking directly in the eyes of an individual, they are viewed as confident, trustworthy and professional.

Hand gestures and facial expression are the second level of transition with a transparent appearance that can be allowed to be seen. Both modes of communication improve the ability to clearly and effectively convey messages. Through skillfully using open and articulate hand gestures, expressive facial expression, greater impact is produced when speaking through engaging the audience more visually and increasing the amount of information provided during the conversation.

As children, many people are taught from an early age that good boys and girls sit together properly with legs and hands folded before them. The desire to limit physical space as children could establish some of the characteristics of the closed identity in adulthood found in the body language. To combat this effect, one can start adopting the characteristics of the body language of the open presence and integrating these ways into their natural state of being. After completion of this behavioral change, it will provide the same non-verbal experiences and signals as their counterparts in the open environment.

To establish the most powerful presence in all interpersonal interactions, the mastery of body language is vital. Individuals without this knowledge are vulnerable to confusion and find their attempts inadequate in expressing their ideas. With the ability to differentiate between different body language styles, anyone can gain the mastery needed to succeed in whatever endeavor they want.

Women's Body Language

Body Language — The language of the Key to Reading Your Body, such as non-verbal movements, postures and expressions, is a topic you've heard of, but you still do not use it. It is still as true as ever and in the dating game, it can certainly give you an advantage.

Much more nonverbally than verbally, you talk. Through body language, women are more verbal and good at interpreting it. Nevertheless, these abilities can be acquired and created by people.

In all kinds of social contexts, there is a lot of very in-depth analysis of body language and a lot of books.

There are two things to your use, however, that you need to concentrate on:

- Observing the body language of people so when you see ten women in a bar you can tell which one is eager to meet you
- Improving your body language signals to ensure that you are friendly, open and congruent, so your anatomy suits what you say.

Body language will help you get a good dating experience. Often only polite women do not initiate an approach — if there is no invitation then rejection is likely. Therefore, by finding out which people are open to approach, you can improve the odds. Learn how to read the body language of women so you know when you have the chance to initiate interaction and when you can move on with trust, or when you are wasting your time and should cut down on your losses and run.

Watching and learning the language which the body so expressly speaks is interesting. Knowing the cues and messages that your body sends out is one of the most important dating skills to learn.

Body Language Basics You need to think about messages from your body and your voice. Focus on her; look at her—her face, her attitude, her relation.

The eyes are said to be the window of the soul, as we have many times iterated. It works in both directions — your eyes represent your innermost thoughts; their eyes show how they feel. You interact more with your eyes than any other part of your body—you can't flirt without communication done with your face.

Give powerful messages to your feet and hands. Are your hands in your or waving wildly about? Are your feet set apart wide open or closed? Are your hands apart or touching? The movements of an open hand show openness, honesty and friendliness.

Your posture will convey a wide range of messages to anyone interested in looking. If you feel defensive or vulnerable, and whether you want to be there, it may show your involvement or otherwise. In your search for a date, all these are important signals given to you.

Her Body Language When trying to read her body language, the most important point to remember is that you can't determine what she is thinking by just seeing one indication of body language. You need to check for indicators of behavior classes. Folded arms can mean that she puts up a barrier. In some cases, this may instead mean that she may be freezing or even that she has spilled something down her blouse and she is trying to cover it up, or it is just the way she always sits down and positions herself. However, it is not how she looks that's significant, but more often it is the most telling shift in body language. When she goes from leaning forward, looking into your eyes and smiling back to leaning back, folding hands, frowning and avoiding eye contact then her mood and demeanor has most certainly changed and it is up to you to understand why and respond accordingly.

Is she interested in you?

Body language is used in two ways to improve your chances of success. First, you need to recognize what women are looking out for a person in a situation. Next, you must interpret the signals that are sent directly to you.

In a social situation, to decide what people you have an opportunity with, first observe how they act. Look around, check out the guys, scan the surroundings? If you do find that you may have an opportunity, this is a sign that they search and are usable. Several key indicators may suggest that she is interested in you and any progress that you may make. Learning to read these signs is the key to improving your performance. Is she staring at you, standing up with her being tilted or leaning towards your direction? Is she laughing or grimacing? Learn how to read her like a book and then know how to respond or behave when you see a green light — a go ahead signal.

Your Body Language

While we are focusing on reading other people's body languages and nonverbal signals, it is important that we also focus on what you are emitting and communicating to other people. Be mindful of the signals that are sent out by every part of your body and posture. Therefore, your physiology is the main area to work on as you approach people. The rule of thumb is to keep eye contact, smile and look polite. Eye contact can be considered aggressive, particularly if you have an unwavering stare! So just keep your eyes for a second or two longer than you usually would when you are finding out if a woman is interested.

Without blinking, do not smile — she might think that you are a lunatic or some weirdo. Also, do not frown — you'll look like you are in agony! Neither are desirable impressions. When you receive a reply, act immediately.

Read People Like Book

Figure out how to read people like a book, and with other people you'll be able to achieve so much more. Once you understand what's going on inside them, you can manipulate them, persuade them and even control them with your mind.

The way you do this is by trying to understand certain patterns of personality and how they organize their inner experience.

You can, for instance, determine if someone is a person who can handle pressure well and even in stressful situations can keep his cool.

There are three key ways in which people respond to stress: mental, decision, or thought. Emotional people are the ones that get plunged into some emotions and can't do anything about it. Choosing people are those who first encounter the emotions, but then choose to separate themselves from them and objectively work through them.

And then some have no emotional response at all — they only respond rationally, objectively, then think things through right away.

One way you can do this is to remind them about a work situation in which they had trouble going through. In reality, emotional people are going to revive the experience to some degree. You might even be sharp enough to hear the emotions in their tone of voice. You may also briefly sport or notice how the muscles in their faces shift, including changes to their body posture or movements.

You could initially see that for people to choose from, but then they go back into a neutral state.

Yet "thinkers" will not go into feelings at all, and they will simply recite the truth. Calculatedly reciting the series of events without much wavering in their tone.

Now, reading this may seem like thinkers are the best type to be in, but it depends on what kind of situation. For example, many of the best cooks in the world seem to be emotional people — and that's no accident. This is because they need to think, feel and experience things to be excellent in their line of work.

Nevertheless, a surgeon should be a thinker rather than a highly emotional person.

And when it comes to counseling jobs or roles where communication skills are needed, "choosers" are usually best because they can react emotionally to the concerns of another person, but they can also see the rational side of it.

So when you are in a situation with high stress, for instance, you might be able to help an anxious person by saying: "Can you imagine how we'll feel about this situation two years from now when we look back on all of this?" This allows them to disassociate themselves from the situation and in that moment, we can become fingers who approach situations with rationale.

Different approaches can work more efficiently depending on what type of person you are speaking to. Often, if you want emotional people to be inspired, use emotional words to make them excited. Using terms such as "mind boggling," "extraordinary," "intense."

They can use phrases for "choosers" such as: "This isn't just exciting and fun, it also makes a lot of sense." And for "thinkers," you are just presenting the hard facts. Mention figures, speak of "clear thinking" and "cold reality."

As you can see, learning to read people like a book takes some practice-but once you get to know it, you can use this ability easily to control other people.

How to Read Body Language

There are two ways in which you can use body language to improve your face-to-face interactions:

1. By studying the person's body language
2. Regulating your body language.

Knowing what others tell you by their nonverbal communication and taking control of the messages you receive can improve your communication skills. The actions and reactions of your body speak louder than words. it is all about knowing what to look for.

Positive nonverbal interaction is generally very effective as an indication of how a person feels without exaggerating gestures. A negative response is indicated by excessive interaction. Nonverbal negative actions are less effective. Actions most often perceived as negative can simply reflect level of comfort, level of energy, or personal diversion. When you notice what you believe is a negative body language, do not jump to conclusions.

If you interact with someone, here are some things to look for:

Posture

If the person you are talking to seems relaxed and breathes naturally, there are usually no big barriers to interaction. There may be cause for concern if their posture is stiff, their movements choppy, their hands clasped in front of them, or they put their palms face down on the table before them.

Language of the skin

A person who is relaxed and open usually maintains uncrossed arms, legs, and feet. it is also a symbol of transparency— and integrity to leave one's jacket closed. Crossing one's arms is often a symbol of defensiveness, and it can show pride or smugness if it is done in conjunction with leaning back. It can simply be a casual gesture if it is done in the sense of an established relationship. Leaning forward is a gesture of curiosity and commitment.

Eye contact

In western cultures, direct eye contact is generally expected. It shows you are interested in the person you are talking to and what you have to say. It builds confidence and strengthens the bond with the person with whom you interact. We generally keep eye contact for about one-third of the time when we talk to someone, looking away from time to time. This means you are lonely or have something to hide to look at someone less. It may express a lack of interest that uncomfortably makes the speaker. We may be irritated by staring at someone for longer periods and, conversely, show enthusiasm and concern. This depends on what follows the prolonged eye contact with other nonverbal communication.

Handshakes, arms and feet

One of the first things you do when you meet someone is to shake hands. What kind of message do you send with your hand shakes? What are the handshakes of others revealing about them? I'm still shocked when I shake hands with someone who's either offering their fingers and treating them as a limp shrimp. it is just as upsetting to get your hand grabbed by what someone seems to be trying to break your hands. Not too strong. Not to frail. Your handshake says a lot about you and you need to make it perfect.

Hands are not for shaking alone. This implies authenticity and truthfulness to reveal them as you act. Movements downward with your hands suggest authority. An individual may make a fist and with an accompanying gesture that means 'atta boy'. For emphasis, one may pound their fist on a table. Clenching one's hands implies hostility and even controlled rage.

Leaning forward or backward

People who lean forward are typically aiming to show interest in whatever or whoever they are listening to. When they lean backward or away from you, it is safe to assume that they either do not agree with what you're saying or are not interested in what you are saying.

Standing and distance from each other

Many people in the U.S. are relaxed just under two feet away from someone they're talking to. it is pulled further apart. Standing closer may be perceived to have sexual overtones and may generate reactions in line with one's approaching feelings. Comfortable distances, like other nonverbal signals, vary dramatically from culture to culture.

Nodding

In response to the remarks of another, nodding shows curiosity and understanding. Bobbing one's head, on the other hand, indicates you are tuned out by the person you are talking to. Head shaking is typically a negative response.

Smiles

Smiles show interest, anticipation, passion, compassion and a variety of other positive reactions. To express a positive response, there is nothing like a genuine smile. On the other hand, frowning or lip narrowing is a hard negative.

Expressions around the eyes

It can be very revealing to say words. One may be perplexed by a wrinkled forehead. Elevated eyebrows may indicate enlightenment. Seeing all the time suggests a lack of confidence. Frequently opening one's mouth makes it seem like you want to interrupt. Try to look at others and their facial expressions to see all the things with one's eyes that can be communicated.

Inspiration

In some cultures, using movements to communicate is more common than others. Talking with one's hands shows openness and engagement, particularly with exposed palms. On the other hand, fidgeting is most often a sign of fatigue, discomfort, nervousness, and caution.

it is touching. It is quick to mis-construct a well-intentioned touch. Be vigilant. If you master the art of nonverbal communication, do not touch. you are going to walk on thin ice.

Watch out for the person you are talking to

Where are they standing and sitting in? How quick do they speak? What's their breathing rate? Try to imitate these signals to establish a relationship faster. Studies have shown that when you match your breathing rate and stance to a person who you are interacting with, they tend to recognise the kinship on a higher level and feel more comfortable.

Note to make

Would you like to let the person you are talking to know you are going to find out what they're saying? Please take notes. it is a great compliment.

Stay congruent with your verbal and nonverbal messages

This is the best way to get your messages through. Furthermore, when, in a friendly voice, you make a hostile remark, the listener will dismiss the animosity and view the message as friendly. And that's because nonverbal contact is better than the words you are talking about.

CHAPTER FIVE

LEARN TO COMMUNICATE WITHOUT TALKING

While my formal degree is in mass communication, I have always considered myself a one-to - one communication graduate. Nonverbal contact also fascinates me, perhaps better known as body language. Evidence follows multiple models and various theories as to what defines human communication, but they all conclude that body language communicates more than half of what we "think." All our parents drilled into our heads the term "actions speak louder than words," which is personified in the selling scenario. The communication between a salesperson and a customer involves giving and receiving wordless messages to and from both parties continuously.

Next time you go to any shop, pay special attention to how (hopefully not "if") a salesperson welcomes you or knows you. Have they looked at you and made eye contact? Have you smiled back? When you approached the counter, did they lean towards you or away from you? How did that little gesture "mean" and what did it say about that salesperson, depending on which? Would you feel like you have faith in them? In setting the stage for continued (or discontinued) communication, these are normal, simple, and somewhat anticipated movements, but also very important. Take a moment today to watch employees from a distance in your shop. Which message would they send to the customer who just came in?

Strengthening relationships by helping you develop your nonverbal skills:

- Understand other people correctly, including the feelings they think and the unspoken signals they convey.
- Send nonverbal signals that suit your words to create trust and consistency in relationships.
- Respond to nonverbal signs showing others you understand, hear, and care.

Unfortunately, most people send misleading or derogatory nonverbal signals without even realizing it. When this occurs, our relationships lose both communication and trust. Trust has always been THE single most important element of a transaction. Lack of that item makes it much harder to close.

I think most people would agree that our nonverbal abilities will possibly be strengthened by everyone. To find the next person you communicate with, one simple exercise is to pay particular attention to the color of their eyes as they talk. Doing so will allow you to research the face of that person and, in general, their eyes. This will, of course, allow you to concentrate even more intensely on what they say and, in effect, convey a message that you are genuinely in tune with what they are trying to communicate.

You can see some very common ones in your showroom here. For example, we're going to use a boat store: > Customer puts their foot on the boat or trailer-this shows a sign of staking out their claim-saying "this is mine" (GOOD SIGN) > Yawning-they're not focused on what you're saying (BAD SIGN) > Feet pointing to the door-watch this after you pose a price — the gesture typically says they're going to get out (BAD SIGN)

Besides, it is important to note that for every single person, body language is not the same. Not even a single action or characteristic tells the whole story. Still the best way to make sure you pick up what they lay down is to ask questions.

The Personality Types That Really Describe Behavior

The workplace is a place where we meet people who are most certainly different from ourselves. It may be filled with people we wouldn't usually hang out from outside the workplace but we have no choice but to see them in the workplace every day.

Therefore, understanding what the ten types of personalities you might meet at work are and how to deal with them is a good idea.

1. The Know It All

For this personality it seems like the individual simply cannot wait to correct you or anyone else in the room. To do so, they can even go out of their way. They possess a lot of knowledge, of course, but you just hate how they always try to show off how intelligent they are.

Solution

The Know It All may be unaware of how annoying people find it when they contradict others. Tell them you understand that they're trying to help, but you'd rather find the answers on your own.

2. The Sniper

Through sarcasm, eye rolls and rude remarks, the sniper excels. They're waiting patiently for a chance to jump on it to make you look poor.

Solution

Provide them with a taste of their own medicine and see how they react. Generally it is their fear that makes them act in this way.

3. The Yes Person

This kind of person does not seem to have the courage to say no. They're doing things to please people all the time.

Solution

Typically the Yes Person is a pleasant person. They can't say no because they want their boss and co-workers to support them. Inform them that you know they're trying to be helpful, but that by handing too many things over and taking on too many, they end up delivering what no one wants.

4. The No Man

The no man is the one person in direct contrast to the yes one. A no person seems to be an expert in saving a group's energy and life. They spread doom and gloom everywhere they go at the sight of new ideas. No one likes the toxicity they exude.

Solution

Explain that their negativity does not render any benefits to themselves or others. This decreases the morale of all the others. Other colleagues can feel negative as well, but like everyone else they get on with their work.

5. The maybe person

They may not seem to be able to make up their mind. They are experts in procrastinating, hoping to avoid decision-making, delay plans, and cause frustration along the way.

Solution

Like the Yes Person, the person may be pleasant. To avoid any conflict, they want others to make decisions for them. Explain that they are only delaying others from getting work done by avoiding making choices.

6. The Grenade

You must always try to stay on the good side of the grenade. When you are in their area, you don't want them to blow. What makes it worse is that at the smallest things, they can sometimes rant uncontrollably and unexpectedly.

Solution

Grenades deep down just want to be respected. That's why they're asking for so much publicity. Explain (although gently) that they will never reach their ultimate goal of gratitude by shouting at people.

7. The Whiner

This individual loves having a good whine. They feel that life is unfair and there never seems to be anything going on their way. They love spreading their suffering and misery to others.

Solution

Empathize with how they feel and then guide them in a different direction. Tell them that instead of moaning with all that energy, it would be better to put it in another field that would help both themselves and others.

8. The Tank

It's never a good idea to get the tank in the way. They exhibit a shockingly aggressive and angry behavior, as if they aim to leave you flattened, psychologically wounded and paralyzed.

Solution

The Tank is a target of publicity like The Grenade and The Whiner. Let them know they won't be protected by their aggressive nature. They will never be accepted by this conduct, it only serves to push people away.

9. The Think They Know It All

This kind of person believes they've got all the answers. A optimistic, arrogant attitude makes people feel they know what they're talking about, but they're just as incompetent as anybody else. While they may seem to share a striking resemblance with the know-it-all, these people only get their confidence or arrogance from things they think they know and are mostly wrong about.

Solution

Explain that, while sounding convincing and compelling, their exaggerations and half truths are only wasting the time of everyone. Let them expressly know that their mode of approach is wrong.

10. The Blank Wall

The Blank Wall (or no-one) seems to think nothing. They have a head in The Matrix that is reminiscent of Neo. With a blank stare and no verbal or nonverbal signals, this type of person appears to be self-restrained.

Solution

The Blank Wall may want to hold themselves or may want to get involved, but I simply suffer from shyness. We seem to be more open than most when faced with a blank wall. Next time you go for a drink or do something after work with your friends, invite the Blank Wall. Most probably they would enjoy it.

UNDERSTANDING PERSONALITY TYPES

1) Evitable Personality

Strong social phobia, hypersensitive to criticism, fear of people, loneliness. When put in low-level occupational positions, where little to no contact and personal interaction is needed, this type of employee can be very efficient and compliant. They are non-threatening and non-demanding, and usually have very few mates, if any. Often because they are too reluctant to react and hate confrontations, they are healthy and eager to take extra work. Such types of people are not antisocial, they are simply intimidated by people, particularly figures of authority. They don't have to be disciplined or micromanaged. Generally, they do all the work on time and make few mistakes. On the downside, "avoiding" workers in leadership positions will not work well and putting them in managerial roles can be a big mistake. They can be exploited and threatened easily and even submerged in illegal practices. These are best suited for jobs requiring minimal communication like clerical, administrative, computer engineering, web-based positions, accounting. They lack human connection and are therefore inspired by basic compassion, encouragement and guidance. We are afraid we are misunderstood or rejected. They're getting along with everyone.

2) Dependent personality

The narcissistic or borderline style director can do well.

They need guidance and direction constantly. Their questions never cease and at every step of the way, they need to be reassured. Because they have to be told constantly what to do, they make good assistants and can become good loyal employees when well educated. Dependent personalities have to be alone with people and terror. They are ready-made followers. Also, this personality type is often worried that they will be hated or rejected if they make wrong choices and not make good leaders. Frustrating and bureaucratic measures that can be used as a guide will need to be enforced on the downside. When left in charge, their indecisiveness and lack of direction will cost a fortune. Approval is their psychological energy, so positive feedback can quickly inspire them. They can make trustworthy, loyal and secure workers.

3) Histrionic temperament

This shows a pattern of constant need for attention, anticipation, passion and enthusiasm. They're outstanding in management, they make great salespeople, speakers, performers, and teachers. Their lives are emotional roller-coasters, they rely on their instincts and go with their instinct, they love to be in front of crowds of people, they're still party life, they're kind and compassionate. Everyone is happier when they are happy but it can be a pleasure or a pain to work with them. They may change their mood suddenly, they may become furious, frustrated, and unhappy. We take it that all personalities can have an attitude that can be dangerous for all or nothing. They can cross the line in some cases and even break the law.

You can make a fortune for your company but it's going to be a roller-coaster ride. Using their strengths: they can take the energy, excitement, imagination and provide as much information and direction as possible. They may need an assistant due to lack of their organizational skills. They must also be constantly reminded of the rules and policies of the organization. With their achievements, they are easily inspired and need little guidance. When assessing their results, be patient and calm as they take it personally. They need to say little to be corrected and make excellent members. That type of person can quickly get angry and frustrated with overly dependent personalities asking too many questions, but will fit well with employee avoidance and type of obsessive-compulsive personality.

4) Borderline Personality

This is the best job I'll ever have and the worst place I've ever served. "They're dangerously unstable, overly emotional, erratic and impulsive. They make decisions that they later regret. You want to avoid hiring this person at all costs if you can detect borderline personality. They expect you to believe what they believe and will get mad if you don't. They go from a high-manic state where they're full of energy, hope, intense joy to rock bottom where they're depressed and suicidal. They can also be described as nuts, neurotic, and sometimes, in need of medical care. This Personality type feels that they have the right to manipulate people and expect them to follow them. They either love you or they hate you. There's no gray area, it's always black or white. These people are volatile and behave based on their current feelings. With stormy romances, drama, mood swings, impulsive spending, substance abuse and poor health, their personal lives are typically messy. Many borderlines can be intelligent and professional and, if you are on their good side, can be a reliable employee. A sense of stability, consistency and encouragement motivates them. They are dysfunctional, so in their personal and professional lives they need someone to rely on. If you can build and give them a sense of security and purpose, you may be one of only a few people in their lives and they can give you all and be one of the best people you've ever had. During their performance evaluation, be calm and compassionate as it is easy to make them feel angry and resentful.

5) Narcissistic personality

These people tend to have feelings of entitlement, do not abide by the rules, think they are more intelligent or better than anybody else, and have a sense of grandiosity. Generally, they feel they're more capable and hated. "It's my way or the highway... I'm unique and deserve to be popular, others don't like me because they're jealous of my talents." such is the thought process of an individual who falls in this category.

They don't fit well within a corporate structure and sometimes make people with their agenda excited and charismatic. They like to feel good at the detriment of others and think it is great for others what is good for them. They tend to take things personally while they can be professional, clever and impressive. If they feel betrayed, it is not unusual for them to indulge in vindictive behaviour. They have a common propensity to control and exploit others for their good. Usually they say more than they are, and they use coercion to undermine others. They also engage in illegal activities and can pose an enormous risk of liability. Although they think they see little use in self-improvement and continuing education around the world. Diplomatically, and often with ass-kissing, they need to be handled carefully. Fragile self-esteem and deep feeling of guilt and inadequacy lie beneath the surface of the superficially bloated ego. Once disciplined or fired, narcissists are likely to resort to malicious lawsuits and abuse. There must be cautious, tactful, respectful and well-documented disciplining and firing.

6) The most dangerous form of antisocial personality in the working environment

These types of people would do whatever it takes to reach their goals without any thought or remorse at the detriment of everything and everyone. It's not always observable and can destroy the entire business. They're going to do absolute minimum work, take advantage of every profit, drive away customers. Ruin prestige, exploit others in their unethical and illegal activities. Many of them become cutthroat businessmen with dubious schemes and greedy ways to go beyond everyone else. They can be aggressive, confrontational, disruptive and impulsive. They would also most likely be disqualified from being employed from the beginning by extensive criminal records.

7)Obsessive-Compulsive Personality

This is a category committed to perfection and attention to detail. At the detriment of their social life, they usually thrive despite their workload. They're scientists, planners, engineers, economists, reporters. With almost any type of personality, they will work well as long as they get the job done because that's their only concern. They are not confrontational or aggressive, and their plan is most often measured, coordinated, and centered. An obsessive compulsive manager would be a good assistant with a dependent personality. They have high expectations on their own and are making demanding managers. It's hoped that everyone will keep up the pace. They believe there is room for change at all times and take their jobs seriously. We also spend too much time "perfecting" the plan as workers, which can cause delays and need to be reminded of deadlines. They are inspired by the sense of accomplishment and give it 110%. Sometimes a sense of direction and deadlines need to be given to them as they can get lost in specifics and be indecisive about the course of the task. Working with it is the simplest and most rewarding type of people. The job is always done and there is no drama.

8) Paranoid personality

This personality type is characterized by extreme lack of confidence and suspicion. They keep their guard, and they don't open easily. This category of people tend to assume that it is not possible to trust people. They believe that the world is full of cruel, greedy people who are going to hurt them and betray them. In general, when they focus on work in complex strategic planning, they may achieve considerable success. People with a paranoid personality are also gifted with technical details, good memory, and strategic goals. Upon gaining confidence and security in their work environment, they will make good leaders. Expect intrusive questioning of the intentions of other individuals and the reasons for their task. They like to hear calm rational explanations and respond well not to guarantees or promises, but reason. Always be honest in giving confidence. Generally, they have sharp cognitive abilities and can immediately smell lies. A sense of entitlement and superiority powers delusional psychology, often in revenge for their subjective feeling of inferiority. They see industry as an area of challenge and have a defensive approach. In your own game, they're ready to beat you, keep their friends close and their enemies closer. You never know what your agenda is. Managing with suspicious workers may be difficult in extreme cases and it can create a stressful and aggressive working environment. If betrayed, you will be pursued and humiliated by the paranoid. Once on the hit list, a painfully plotted way out, your fate is sealed. We assume that their fault is nothing.

9) Passive-Aggressive Personality

This type believes that life is not fair, nothing is their fault, something bad happens to them even if they do everything wrong, they are a victim and they always have "perfectly reasonable" explanations. They never take responsibility or behave like a party that has been hurt. Through their job, they are passive practitioners of procrastination, and they use "self-handicapping" methods that they use as an excuse for not doing work. They are hostile, malicious, and can engage in sabotage, corporate espionage, malicious whistle-blowing, and can sink into any company. We were eligible to sue for civil law. Be vigilant about firing that type of person, report and convey the reasons for this decision, and provide a face-saving way to leave the company. Eventually, this person will become the burden of someone else. To stop more lawsuits, be vigilant of guidelines.

The bottom line: Hiring competent professionals who can get along well and get the job done to create an ideal work atmosphere. Carefully screen the candidates to remove any apparent troubled people with substance abuse records, criminal history, litigation, poor record quality, or financial issues. They're just going to be troublesome and a waste of time. Hire the right people— they're the ones that will make you a good manager and help the company grow.

COMMON NON-VERBAL MISTAKES

Our body is our most valuable asset, allowing us to do everything from building houses from the ground up to the taste of a fine wine's most subtle flavors. For everything, our body has complex systems; breathing, feeding, speaking, even talking. What most people fail to realize is that our bodies are constantly showing clear signs of what is happening to our minds. These can be good, good to say the least, for our contact, for our contact.

Some of us, especially women, are interested in subtle signs in body language. But some aren't. Some may interpret the signs better than others (maybe through self-training or just plain experience), which usually means they can transmit the same signs as easily as possible. This seems almost unfair to someone who is not as aware of their non-verbals. Read the following for those of you who may just understand the value of non-verbal communication or want to gain a better handle on their social life.

These are some of the most common non-verbal "errors."

1. Shifty eye contact

This is one of the most common mistakes I see today, it's also one of the most IMPORTANT things to be managed. Touch with shifty eyes. Eye contact is a huge asset to have under your command, it can tell someone whether you are secure in your interaction (and your skin) or not, while it can also show people that you are someone that can be taken seriously. Shifty eye contact can make you look like they're not comfortable, insecure, socially awkward, inexperienced, have a lack of self-confidence (which ultimately causes a lack of confidence from others) and the list goes on. If two lions face each other in the eyes, they must look at each other. We measure the "power" of the opposite, and we decide their position. The alpha is confirmed by the best eye contact while the shifty, soft eye contact confirms the beta. Nevertheless, this often means death or exile for a lion. Death or exile normally won't happen in our present world... But that doesn't mean it doesn't matter. Strong eye contact means strong character, someone who believes in their values and someone who is not afraid of who they are.

Effective approach

Take note of your eye contact with others from this moment on. See how some people change it. Take note of the modifications. Focus on the conversation on your eye contact. Keep a lot of eye contact, but it's not a competition for the stars. At first, it may seem like knives shooting from the eye contact into your eyes; it's going to go away. You may also make eye contact so much that it is odd and uncomfortable, it will also subside; you will finally have a relaxed, normal connection with your eyes. Remember how the reactions of peoples change over time.

2. Closed body language

Whether you are a man or a woman, your body language can give similar signals (depending on the type of contact in which you are). Closed language of the body is a great gift for lack of social skills. Note, you're inaccessible to those around you, you're not open to change or new experiences. You may be, but otherwise your body will say. A person in a conversation that is closed to you might look a little odd, almost anti-social. You might like they're hiding from you, or maybe even scared of you, or more specifically, scared of what you might think. It goes both ways, what does the language of your body say? Clear body language indicates that someone is lacking in terror, that they are not afraid or ashamed to express themselves. The language of the open body is often viewed as welcoming, and also makes contact with the other person more relaxed. Closed as opposed to open.. What does your body say? Closed arms are a sure sign of closed body language as arms can be opened freely on your sides or hips. Hands in pockets that are locked, vs. hands that are free from pockets... Get it? Get it?

Effective approach

Try opening it up the next time you're in conversation, if you're a body language shut. Opening up can feel like revealing yourself at first, perhaps leaving you vulnerable. Yet relax, there's no risk that a spear will be fired at your head. Relax, open up, and see the reaction difference.

3. Nervous jits

Does anyone ever see someone anxiously shift their weight from one foot to another? Or maybe (a lot of times) pick their fingernails? Scratch the eyes, scratch the nose, giggle their keys in the hands / pockets? The list continues. These are all nervous jit cases. Some are VERY obvious, and some are less apparent, you can usually tell when someone is anxious. You can imagine what somebody's doing.

"Why are you so anxious, we're talking about it?"

Get it? Nervous jits tell you a lot of negative things, even to your advantage. Take a nervous jit's mental note and start working it out of your mind. If you have a jiggling key problem, you might want to hold it out of your mouth and your hands out of your pockets. Eliminating it is easy once you can identify them.

Active approach

Take your anxious jits ' mental note. Also, you'll interact with the absence of anxious jits from now on. It may take a while, hold it, you'll soon find out it's not that nerve-wrecking.

There are many more non-verbal "errors," but try to take note of your personal "errors" for now. Are you any of the above? If so, focus on the exercises I mentioned above for the active approach and see them trickle back one by one. In my experience, these are the greatest breakers of social interactions. It refers in general to corporate and technical contact. Employers look at these during interviews, as well as a number during dating. Remember your customs.

CHAPTER SIX

BUILDING YOUR LISTENING SKILLS

We also connect by email in our world today. This is a verbal and non-vocal form of communication. In other words, to communicate with each other, we use written words, but not our voice.

Communication is verbal or emotional when speaking to someone on the phone. Hearing the voice of someone is an added aspect of interaction and is often considered more important and easier to understand.

We experience verbal and vocal interaction when we meet someone in person, and we have the added advantage of non-verbal and non-vocal communication. This means that the elements of interaction go beyond what comes out of their mouths and instead, what is exhibited on their body or face. It ensures that we can track the expressions and movements on their faces. We can also see the orientation of their body, their stance, how they move in their personal space, whether or not they make eye contact, and even their appearance. Such non-verbal / non-vocal findings can give us a huge amount of information. That is as long as non-verbal / non-vocal interaction is compatible with vocal / verbal communication. In other words, to completely ascertain that what a person is uttering is genuine, their words must match the energy andessage being passed off through non-verbal channels.

Imagine an excited person saying, "I'm happy to be here" with a big smile on his face, rapidly and loudly. He uses his non-verbal / non-vocal signals to convey what he thinks, what he wants, what his desires truly are.

Here, we are emphasizing the verbal / vocal message as well as the non-verbal / vocal interaction because it includes the intonation used by the person speaking, the sound of the voice, the rhythm, the rate at which they are speaking, and even if they are pausing or sighing. Generally, this is the way people interact and with keen attention being paid by the listener, it is very possible to gain more from an interaction.

Now, imagine a person with a poor posture saying, "I'm glad to be here," eyes down, tone quiet, and voice unenthusiastic. He also says, "I'm so glad to be here," but this leads to confusion as there is a difference between his vocal / non-verbal message and his vocal / verbal response. If you are a keen listener who pays attention to the non-verbal channels, you will quickly note that there is a disconnect between what he is saying and what he is feeling. It is not a secret that individuals Do not always say what they mean or mean what they say. Hence, it's not always easy to know what a person feels for sure.

Communication can be very complex, as you can see, including written words, spoken words, facial expression and movements, and sound, pitch, and speed tone. Start fine-tuning and improving your listening skills by listening to verbal, non-verbal, auditory, and non-vocal communication with your ears and eyes. This is one way to optimize your interactions and make the most of the information you gather from them.

HOW TO DISCOVER CONFIDENCE

We must all feel confident at all times. Especially when we need it, it's a bit hard to regain faith in ourselves and sometimes, other people. There are simple activities that can be done to get your confidence back on track as soon as you need it, whenever and however. **There are seven ways to be confident:**

Watch Your Attitude

This may not sound like a partnership with the confidence we are talking about, but the way you are sitting or standing can send some messages to people around you. If that message expresses trust, you will receive a positive response from others, which will, of course, raise your confidence. So start watching your sit and standing to prove your confidence.

The best way to do this is to focus on your posture, demeanor, and resting face. Many times, some people have a "resting face" that tends to be mean-looking. They might not intend to look so, but because they have taken their minds off their outer attitude, it comes into play. Whether you are standing, sitting, or doing anything else, build the habit of subconsciously paying mind to your attitude.

Associate with people with confidence and positive thinking

It is often said that man is a social animal. This saying has never held truer than this. Neighborhood has an enormous impact on somebody. When you tend to associate with low-confidence people, complainants, and pessimists, no matter how much esteem you have, it will slowly but surely dissipate and be pulled to suit your neighborhood and the energy you have surrounded yourself with. When, on the other hand, you are surrounded by people full of happiness and trust, it will also create a positive environment that will bring benefits for you.

Remember if you feel confident

If you have ever felt confidence once, it is certainly not impossible to feel it again. Remembering the moment when you felt confident and in control can make you feel and help put a sense of confidence in mind. Here, you are simply relying on and calling upon your memories to remind you what it felt like to have confidence. This reminder gives you the push you need and voila, confidence!

Exercise

The trick is to exercise as often as possible whenever you want to feel the confidence. You can even take your bed with you. You won't have trouble displaying confidence whenever necessary with a qualified skill.

Know yourself

Think about yourself and all the stuff you know you can do well. If you are having trouble doing this, note people's feedback — what they're saying. Do they think you are doing well? Do they enjoy any services or value that you offer? Writing all of this is a good idea until you need to see it again to boost your self-confidence anytime inspiration is needed.

Do not be too harsh on yourself

Many people say that your greatest critics may very well be yourself. It is important that you are mindful of this natural human tendency and work towards making it work for you and not against you. Do not be dismissive of yourself; you have got to be your best friend. But when a friend is going through a difficult situation, you will not want to get involved in the problem, so you are going to get your emotional drain, right? You Do not want that, of course. Positive talk can turn into the best weapon for improving self-confidence, so make sure you set the habit, Do not let others ' problems make you too bad.

Do not be afraid to take a chance

If you are a risk-taker, you will find that this action will build trust in yourself. However, this action also works well to reduce your anxiety about things you do not know, plus it will boost confidence considerably.

Creating Effective Visual Displays

If you use the same ideas over and over again, designing attractive displays can become tedious. No matter how wonderful a show may be, consumers may lose interest if you use it too much, staff will not be excited, and your business may start looking dull. Use these ideas to return the retail displays to life. Organize the shop for optimal sales. Get prepared for the holiday season and make your shop more effective than ever before.

It's not just how important it is to see a show. You can create a complicated template with purses of the Eiffel tower. It would be fun, but it wouldn't sell any purses necessarily. The show style must conform to the theme of the product you are promoting. For example, distress washed jeans and retro t-shirts might show a style of rock-n-roll, loosely stacked on a table, or worn by a mannequin wearing a hat and head-set. For a designer suit that is best presented on a wooden hanger or more formal mannequin, that may not fit so well.

If the clothes you are selling are casual, you can be imaginative. However, you shouldn't forget that maintaining your image, building customer trust, gaining attention, and organizing things are critical. Thinking about it is a lot, but not very difficult to get.

Start by arranging and showing items where consumers can see them. Crowded, jumbled racks are an inefficient way to go. Using a system like a gridwall or a Slatwall system will keep things very organized and provide your customers with incredible views of your products. These are particularly effective in optimizing the small retail spaces you see in shops and malls.

Hang enough front-facing things to convey your look to your displays. Alternate textures and designs or create interesting patterns using colors. You can use your imagination, but be careful not to take note of the items you endorse. In the center of your gridwall, if your red clothing all forms a star, it will certainly catch your attention! But did it directly lead all of your customers past your promotional display? Make sure you are putting displays around big attention getters to see them.

CHAPTER SEVEN

THE COMMUNICATING CONFIDENCE GUIDE

Strong-minded people have faith and can express that sense of trust to others even when they may not feel confident in themselves. What separates them from shy people is their body language, and it is this posture that is essential to send the right message or signal to others. This aura of faith that experts are immediately released is crucial in all areas of life from business negotiations to attracting other people.

The more relaxed you are, the more confident you are, and the more the confidence that people have in you. Confident people have that 'something' about them that makes things turn to their favor, and they always seem to have the lucky breaks in life. What other people do not realize is that achieving this highly desirable value is not too difficult.

The key to being a confident person is to act honestly before others even though you may have your own personal and private issues inside. Bluffing with a poor poker hand and playing on stage are perfect examples of how much more relaxed you are behaving the more people see you as the real deal.

Habits are another field that separates trustworthy people from shy people. Empowering habits will improve your life no-end, and as a result, you will boost your faith by developing the right habits for thinking and communicating. With your newly found faith in your ability, the change in your life will leave you ecstatic.

Through positive thinking, confidence can be expressed. By displaying a much more positive disposition, practicing your confidence through remembering memories or interactions of trust from your history will show this in your physiology. At the same time, the higher your level of physical confidence, the more confident your reasoning will be. Note, as a single entity, the body and mind still work together in tandem.

Extra trust can be gained by looking at how people behave with confidence. Research their self-confident walk and gestures, consider their body posture and wonder about their thoughts. You can create an identity for the 'ideal' individual by doing this. Take your ideal person's identity and make use of the features you have found.

Ignore the negative body language cues that some people give out to exude trust. Slouching, avoiding eye contact or hanging one's head is an action that you should stop as it shows a lack of self-control and submissiveness. This also refers to angry or panicky behavior, which means that you are not in control of the situation. Throughout stress situations, optimistic people are cool and relaxed and are usually chosen as leaders as they have the right qualities to solve any problems. Therefore, you have to try to adopt the qualities of a leader to meet those of a positive one.

Instead of pointing fingers, gesturing and accusing others, people who are fully confident tend to seek solutions to any problems they face while showing a positive attitude towards the outside. Trust is correlated with an intensity which explains why it attracts others. Imagine going to a job interview trying to sell yourself and you don't have much faith in yourself. If you do not believe in yourself, how can a potential employer believe in you? You will ultimately become a much more confident person simply by acting confidently.

When You Betrayed by Body Language

If you've read and retained anything about body language, you're likely to have heard that 90% of interaction is non-verbal. The real source of this slightly distorted statistics, which concluded in his 1971 study Silent Messages that interaction in each conversation is 7% letters, 38% voice sound and 55% facial expression. Consequently, the body language is born in 90% (or rather 93%) of all contact. Nonetheless, believing that most contact is made by body language would be incorrect. We typically don't contradict what people say in everyday life, so what is fascinating about body language and how helpful body language is concerning what is being said.

In people with advanced dementia, physical appearance is an important factor in pain assessment due to the decreased ability to communicate verbally, but in almost all situations, a nurse would not rely on how a patient behaves to determine how much pain a person has, they would ask the patient. Similarly, if someone sits crossed with their arms and legs and looks annoyed on their face, you probably won't be talking to them. Body language is 100% of contact in this situation, but the only way to make sure is to talk to them. Through revealing your emotions and mood, body language betrays you, yet it is your words and their interaction with your body language that is central to your communication.

Notwithstanding, the essential elements of body language in interaction, non-verbal communication is quite limited without the verbal component of communication. It's the combination of words and body language that betrays you, especially when you don't suit what you say and how you behave. Mehrabian defined congruence or continuity between body language and words as a crucial element of non-verbal communication study; finding when the words and actions of an individual fit or fail to match.

But surely you have nothing to worry about if a person hasn't learned body language? Until body language books existed, people picked up on the signals without being fully aware of what they were picking upon. You won't need a book on body language to help you read the signs when someone says they're happy but don't look happy. Even if the person you spoke to didn't read the books, your body language is highly likely to betray you.

When you deal with other people daily, what you need to be concerned with is not what you talk, but how you behave in response to what you say. If you're saying enthusiastic things, your body language can be all chaotic and excited, but when you're lying, the situation is different.

But if you tell the truth, why do you want the language of the body to be fake? The response is that we're only people. Sometimes when we tell our partner's nice things or talk to our bosses, we're just too lazy or just not involved. We can talk about the one thing we think is the world's most interesting or exciting thing, but if we're hungry, or exhausted, or sick, or just having a bad day, the words we use may be excited, but our body language may betray us.

How are you falsifying it? Many experts say that you can't manipulate the language of your body. If you've read' top ten signs she likes you' or' how to tell if he's cheating,' this is good news. But if you're trying to make yourself look good then it might be an issue.

So, what are we going to do? The simple answer is to increase the difference between what we say and the language of our body. In two ways, we are growing incongruence: the first thing we can do is, to be frank. If you're not, do not try to sound too excited. Do not try to compensate if you feel tired by being overly excited. You may be excited about it but do not overdo it. You don't lie to them if you disagree with someone. Only stop responding directly to them as much as possible. So when your friend or girlfriend asks "Do I look fat in this?" response with "You look great" or "You look good in that dress" and then try to change the subject. You're probably lying, whether you say yes or no. Don't answer the question, therefore. Don't avoid the topic, but don't answer the question directly.

The second thing we can do is learn how you think and do something else. Congruence is about consistency; you should be able to make interpreting them hard and thus break congruence when you cast doubt on the continuity of the symbols.

Although telling the truth can be a delicate matter, disturbing your body language's congruence would allow you to think about how you feel and learn something about body language. It doesn't require a lot of details, but you should be mindful that body language is usually considered to function in clusters, so what you're doing with your arms is only important when it's about your face's expression and how you're standing. You will want to break down the clusters of your acts and potentially interrupt congruence when you need to make sure that someone doesn't read anything about you from your body language.

Body language areas to concentrate on: facial expressions: if you're feeling bored or you're showing interest, if you're comfortable showing a little disappointment, if you don't have to say something, make it like you want to tell. If anyone you talk to offers you the opportunity to speak and you don't, they're going to start challenging their perception of you.

Eye contact:

Failure to maintain contact with the eye indicates a lack of interest or frustration. Aggressively sustained eye contact indicates another person's desire to conquer. Measure your thoughts and desires and change contact with your eyes accordingly.

Touch:

The actual touch demonstrates the attraction. In a dating situation, if a woman starts touching another male, however innocently, she shows interest in them. Avoid touching improperly. Inappropriate touching in the workplace is nothing more than a hug. Do touch in relationships between people. You may feel strained, but that embrace will be enjoyed by your partner.

Arms and legs:

All kinds of things about you are revealed by your stance. Two things to be mindful of our arms and legs pointing and body posture open or closed. We also show interest in someone by pointing to them with our arms and legs. If we're not interested or eager to go, we could point our limbs to the door in an attempt to be ready when it's time to go. The distinction between crossed arms and legs and uncrossed arms and legs is the open or closed body pose on a very basic level. "I'm not interested or listening," says the closed body. An open body says the opposite.

Voice tone:

how are you behaving normally? Are you a fast loudspeaker, a very quiet speaker? When you're mad, think about how you sound. Don't get taken away too much. If you're just tired, you don't want the boss to feel you're violent, so think about size, pace, tone, and infuse a little emotion with your speech.

The language of your body will deceive you. The uncontrollable incongruity between how you behave and what you say will say something you don't want. Talk about what you'd like to do and how you think, and then do something completely different. A minor noise goes a long way.

Disrupting the language of the body can be hard work and you wouldn't want to do anything all the time. If you use it on an exceptionally perceptive buddy regularly, they will pick up your cues and see your plan through. You can fight back against the deceit of body language when you interrupt congruence if you feel uncertain.

Understanding The Subconscious Mind

I addressed the different roles that the conscious mind, unconscious and subconscious mind and supra-conscious mind play in our chapter called "The Subconscious Mind-Understanding The Power And Potential Inside."

I want to speak about how we harness the energy of the subconscious mind in this post. When a guy started his self-awareness quest, he had developed an idea that the subconscious mind was like a "gremlin" that sabotaged his life. He had chosen to accept the notion that the subconscious mind was this all-powerful "thing" that contained all the past failures of his life and pulled up all the fear and restricting values that he had as he tried to create a fresh and empowered image of me.

He had generated this illusion somewhere along the line that the subconscious mind was in reality, his mind with a very specific agenda. He saw it as part of his heart, containing all of his "truths." The dirty little secrets he'd never tell others. But when he wanted to become more than what he was at the moment, they would always come up and somehow stop his advancement dead in his tracks. And indeed, because he had developed the subconscious mind interpretation as something that would hold him back... It was his truth.

What he learned as he advanced in his understanding of human behavior and psychology is that a subconscious mind is simply a tool we were not taught how to use effectively. An analogy he's heard many times is that "the human brain is the most efficient supercomputer on the planet. We've just never got the user's manual." Without the "user's manual," we've let our minds run rampant, with little to no real direction, and more to the point, very limited knowledge of how to fix any of the issues created by this lack of understanding.

When we look at the subconscious mind as a simple tool, not an agent with good or bad intentions or some "master plan" to guide our lives, we will begin to understand how to use it to our advantage.

One of the things that helped him better understand how to handle his subconscious was to figure out that our unconscious mind phrases were like a storage unit, similar to a hard drive on your desktop. Information is collected and processed simply by our different senses. The difference is that when the information is stored in your subconscious mind, like a database, it is "indexed" so that when you need specific information from your conscious mind, there is a way to retrieve it.

The first thing that helped him to understand this machine metaphor was that his subconscious mind was just a device to do a job. So that led to the question, if it's just an instrument, what in the past has given it so much "destructive" power? More research helped him understand that the unconscious mind is not placing a value judgment on the information given to him. It doesn't look at the information, and it goes, "Hmm... it's great, it's bad, it's right, and it's wrong." It does not even decide how it is handled. It takes the information given to it just like a machine... Just like it's given. And just like a machine, your subconscious would simply accept the error as what you meant it to be given when you make an error in the information you give it.

Now that he knew that the subconscious mind was merely processing the data, he had to tell me what decides what knowledge is being remembered? We have collected and stored every experience we have ever had in our unconscious mind. When we advance in our lives, these interactions are accessible to us as guides and tools. And here's where the absence of a user's manual becomes an issue.

Because we have not been taught how to exploit these resources properly, we generally do "the best we can" based on the resources we have. We learned that "You get what you're focused on," but we weren't taught how to channel our attention in ways that allow us to get what we want.

Through learning how to guide our conscious mind, we will begin to gain access to the real abilities that our unconscious "library" has at our fingertips. So what does he mean specifically when he refers to how we focus our conscious mind? In the end, we have the freedom to choose what we are focused on. It is said that we receive more than 10 million bytes per second of data. And as a matter of survival so working capacity, our conscious, unconscious, and supra-conscious all have specific information reserved for them. We have also been given the ability to filter the data that we take by taking the specific information that we concentrate on to our "dominant" focus area, while the rest of the information is processed without paying much attention to it.

As an example, at this very moment, you are being transmitted terabytes of data through your different senses.

If you had to process all this data at one time at a conscious level, you'd be in an "overloading state." So there are things you're paying particular attention to right now that are kept as the "dominant details" we mark as your "goal" or the information you're concentrating on right now. If you're reading this section, he'd think there are several items you're focused on right now. When you read the words on this page, the computer screen, the words on this page, your inner voice. There may be other sounds around you that you know about, but they aren't just as much of your focus.

Yet there's a lot of other things going on that you're aware of, even though they're not your current focus.

The room temperature on the body, for example, and the difference in that temperature where the skin is uncovered, and where it is dressed. Perhaps the pressure of your clothing's waistband, the pressure of your arm or wrist as it lies on your table or lap. What about things that you didn't pay attention to before that could happen? Perhaps a fan running in the background, or perhaps an outdoor conversation. A car's tone going by. What about your right butt cheek's tension on the chair on which you sit.

Now let him ask a question as he started to mention these things, and you shifted your attention to them, did you become more conscious of what he described? Have these things begun to happen magically as he described them? Or have you simply shifted your attention to make them part of your dominant focus?

Then we can better understand how our attention controls our subconscious mind by recognizing how we regulate our concentration. Who guides our attention specifically? Questions. The specific questions you are constantly asking yourself are deciding your concentration. Most of these things happen so quickly, and you don't even consider them so subtly. For example, when he raised the topic of room temperature against your body, and the difference in that temperature where the skin is exposed, versus where it is clothed; you immediately asked yourself a question... More than probably, "Did he feel the temperature in the room against his body, and the difference in the temperature in which the skin is visible, as opposed to the temperature in which it is covered with clothes." In asking the question, you answered your question and changed your mind.

The information was collected and stored by your unconscious, you only needed to retrieve it to guide your attention. For many of us, this is the problem. Instead of choosing where we focus, we allow external influences or repetitive patterns to determine what we focus on.

CONCLUSION

Feeling comfortable in any social interaction is the most important element. Girls will easily pick up on it, and it is the best way to get them attracted by hands down. Unfortunately, through a lengthy series of positive experiences and results, trust is something you build up over a considerable amount of time, even years.

Thankfully for you, there are some things you can do to give the impression that you are instinctively confident and relaxed around women, even though you haven't built it up since childhood.

There's also a complex — the more popularly known saying, "fake it until you make it." The more of these characteristics you display, the more they become part of you, and you will begin to feel more comfortable naturally.

At first, it will make you feel uncomfortable as these are habits you are not used to. But what do you think? Guys with girls who are great do not even care about this material, and you won't have to either long enough.

Yet remember: you do not want to be rude or cocky, optimistic. Here are some useful pointers:

1. Presume Attraction: You should presume that she is already attracted to you when you first talk to a woman. do not pretend to believe it alone. Trust it.

Believe it. It will make it much more congruent with everything you do and say. Confident guys think they are drawn to every woman already.

2. Body Language: If you speak to her, use deliberate gestures. do not flail about your neck. do not be mad, even though you are nervous. Becoming an unconscious habit may take some time, but at the start, you need to be self-conscious about your movements. Do not turn your head around when someone says something to you to look at them. Use deliberate, purposeful movements.

3. Keep your shoulders back and head up as you run. do not look down on the ground. do not be afraid to make eye contact with people around you (and do not look down instantly when you are making eye contact, that's a sign of submission).

4. do not worry about taking up space. Stand about one foot-and-a-half apart with your hands. You can make sure that you take up as much space as you need to be relaxed even when you sit down. Think of "male alpha."

5. Tonality: Also, you need to speak slowly and deliberately when you talk. Suppose they're interested in hearing what you've got to say. Project your voice, but do not cry out for attention in any way. Do not ask if she agrees if you make statements. you are not saying "right?" or "you know?" It makes you look nervous whereas you

should be oozing confidence in what you know —
here, you must be certain that what you are saying
is correct and you must be sure that you know what
you are talking about.

6. You shouldn't handle any contact with a woman at
the same time as a business meeting (except, you
know, if it is a business meeting). So keep it light,
keep it fun. Laugh, but not the ones of your own.
you are all jokes that need a smirk. Do not answer it
too quickly when she asks you a question, and do
not give more details than is needed. Never
overcompensate for your shortcomings or
insecurities.

When you start incorporating these components as part of
your identity, girls are going to start picking them up. The
awkwardness can take days, weeks, or even months to go
away. But it is going to eventually, and you are going to
stop pushing these habits.

These are the bare necessities you should start thinking like
a guy whose natural confidence attracts women
automatically.

Remember: when you change your way of thinking, you
are going to change your way of thinking.

MIND MASTERY SERIES

If you have come to this Book without having read the previous parts, I suggest you do so in order to have an overall reading. Below is the correct titles, if you would like to search for them on Amazon and/or Audible:

DARK PSYCHOLOGY

HOW TO MANAGE YOUR EMOTIONS AND INFLUENCE PEOPLE WITH PERSUASION. PENETRATES THE SUBCONSCIOUS MIND OF ANYONE THROUGH SECRET MANIPULATION TECHNIQUES

SECRET MANIPULATION TECHNIQUES

HOW SUBLIMINAL PSYCHOLOGY CAN PERSUADE ANYONE BY APPLYING DARK PNL IN REAL-LIFE. UNDERSTANDING TACTICS & SCHEMES TO INFLUENCE PEOPLE AND CONTROL THEIR EMOTIONS

HOW TO ANALYZE PEOPLE WITH DARK PSYCHOLOGY

A SPEED GUIDE TO READING HUMAN PERSONALITY TYPES BY ANALYZING BODY LANGUAGE. HOW DIFFERENT BEHAVIORS ARE MANIPULATED BY MIND CONTROL

Do not go yet; One last thing to do…

*If you enjoyed this book or found it useful I'd be very grateful if you'd post a short review on **Amazon**. Your support really does make a difference and I read all the reviews personally so I can get your feedback and make this book even better.*

Thanks again for your support !

Made in the USA
Coppell, TX
17 March 2021